PREPARED *to be* GOD'S VESSEL

HOW GOD CAN USE AN OBEDIENT LIFE TO BLESS OTHERS

HENRY BLACKABY

and

CARRIE BLACKABY WEBB

OLIVER
NELSON

TM

THOMAS NELSON PUBLISHERS®
Nashville

A Division of Thomas Nelson, Inc.
www.ThomasNelson.com

Published in Nashville, Tennessee, by Thomas Nelson, Inc.

Nelson Books titles may be purchased in bulk for educational, business, fund-raising, or sales promotional use. For information, please e-mail SpecialMarkets@ThomasNelson.com.

Library of Congress Cataloging-in-Publication Data

Prepared to be God's vessel : how God can use an obedient life to bless others / [edited by] Henry Blackaby and Carrie Blackaby Webb.
    p. cm.
Includes bibliographical references (p.   ).
ISBN: 0-7852-6207-5 (hardcover)
    1. Obedience—Religious aspects—Christianity. 2. Obedience—Biblical teaching. 3. Mary Blessed Virgin, Saint. 4. Christian Women—Religious Life. I. Blackaby, Henry T., 1935– II. Webb, Carrie Blackaby.
BV4647.O2P74 2006
248.4—dc22   2005036831

Printed in the United States of America

1 2 3 4 5 QW 10 09 08 07 06

*To my daughter, Carrie, who worked so faithfully
with me in writing this book, and to my mother, Jennie,
who devotedly taught me to walk with the Lord.*
—HENRY BLACKABY

*To my husband, Wendell, who sacrificially gave of his time,
love, and support so that this book could be written. And to my
two children, Elizabeth and Joshua, who, with their father,
are my greatest blessings from the Lord.*
—CARRIE BLACKABY WEBB

CONTENTS

CONTENTS

INTRODUCTION

Seeing a Life from God's Perspective

MARY WAS A SIMPLE, ordinary woman who was chosen by God for an extraordinary role in His salvation plan. God chose, empowered, and equipped her to unfold His activity throughout her life. He was about to provide salvation to the world and set in motion His plan to send His Son to live among us. Why would God choose this peasant girl and entrust her with the raising of our Savior? What can we learn from God's activity in her life that applies to us today?

When we look at Mary's life from our limited perspective, we see an ordinary girl, living a simple life. God, however, saw a pure heart that was ready to obey Him. According to the genealogies in Matthew 1 and Luke 3, God had been preparing for such a heart in Mary for centuries. God had a much bigger involvement in her life than she knew. But it becomes obvious that from her earliest days she had a pure and obedient and faithful heart toward God. God had prepared her for this, and she responded with humility and obedience. When God chose uniquely to come to her, she was ready. God's choices are not "accidental," but eternally purposeful.

This sense of an eternal and divine purpose for our lives is what we will seek to unfold for each of us, as we see Mary's life from God's perspective.

Throughout Mary's life, she had many roles: a peasant, a wife, a homemaker, a teacher, a mother—and she was also the mother of God's Son. God can use any woman, regardless of her status or abilities, if her heart is fully committed to respond in faithful obedience.

Christian women today are struggling to know God's will for their lives. They want to be God's servants but often don't know how to respond or how to find the next step. Sometimes they can find themselves pressured by the world and encouraged to assert themselves and their rights. Women are told to seek a career outside the home to express their independence, and they can also feel pressured from within the Christian community to discover their gifts and establish their ministry.

All of these pressures, both in the world and the church, are real and sometimes frightening—if a person does not search the Scriptures. We must know how God purposed for us to be fully His, in the center of His eternal will for our lives, and therefore to be complete in Christ (Col. 2:9–10).

As each stage of Mary's life unfolds, we will seek to apply the truths revealed for the Christian woman today. We will encourage every woman to expect, accept, and faithfully live out God's revealed will for her, in her personal life and in her family. Understanding and applying God's truths as revealed in this study will enable us to handle confusion, challenges, friendships, sorrows—and finish well, with a real sense of fulfillment!

Each of us must carefully study what Jesus meant when He said, "These things I have spoken to you, that My joy may remain in you, and that your joy may be full" (John 15:11). The world gives no thought to God or His divine purposes. Yet all too often, we as God's people look to the world to satisfy our need for fulfillment and purpose. Instead, we should be encouraged to search the Scriptures to find and experience God's fullness for life. This book will seek to reveal the eternal purposes of God for the fullness of life for every person. Many of the questions we raise relate to choices we each must make between God's ways and the world's ways. It is only by God's ways that we will ever find real fullness of life.

Studying together in groups is helpful. It is especially good to encourage new believers just out of the world and the maturing believers who need teaching and careful instruction in God's Word. Reading through a study on your own is always beneficial too, as you can take as much time as you need to work through God's truths. God, by creation and by redemption, made us interdependent. We need each other for the fullest understanding of God's Word. As you study Scripture with others, listen carefully to God giving you fresh and timely insights you could not have gained by your solitary study. You will notice Mary's interdependence with others who God placed with her, and you will see the insights God gives her through others for her fuller understanding of God's activity in her life.

Mary was young. She was inexperienced. She was a peasant. She did not have a formal education. To her culture and her society, she was nothing special. Yet God chose her to be His vessel and affect eternity! This assignment was difficult, but God made many provisions to guide Mary and help her at the pivotal points of her life. Early on, He provided older believers such as Elizabeth and Zacharias, Simeon, and Anna to strengthen and encourage her in her faith. He gave her faithful companions along the way and provided John, who filled the duties of an eldest child when Mary's husband and Jesus had both died. God also gave her the joy of seeing the early church and observing many come to faith through her Son—just as God promised her. Mary's relationship to the Father was learned through walking a difficult path with Him and experiencing His faithfulness throughout her life. She had to choose to live obediently, even through the extreme pain she would endure.

This is not simply a biographical study of Mary's life. We are using Mary's example of faithfulness and commitment to encourage and strengthen Christian women, knowing that God is continuing to look for a pure heart that He can use today.

Sadly, Mary's life and her assignment by God have been widely misunderstood. Yet her role as God's "highly favored one" and her experience as God's servant are critical for us to know and apply to our lives today. We can learn so many things from Mary's life and example. Together through this study, we can come to a clearer understanding of how to prepare our lives to be vessels through which God will bless others.

In many ways, this book is also a collection of stories. God is using His people for His glory in so many ways today that we wanted you to have a small taste of how God is continually at work around us. Does God still use women for His glory? Yes. Are women playing a major role in God's work today? Yes. To help us draw a clearer picture of how God is continuing to use women today, we have decided to include some practical examples of women who have had their lives touched by God. These are everyday people who come from different backgrounds and different experiences, who have made the choice of keeping God first in their lives. Most of these women you have never heard of, but they have each, through their obedience to their Lord, changed history in God's Kingdom!

We hope the testimonies of God's servants are as much a blessing to you as they have been to us. We have also included many personal examples from both of our experiences to help apply what we've learned about Mary into our own lives.

I (Henry) have chosen our daughter, Carrie, to write with me. She is doing in her life what together we are urging you to experience as you live out the will of God in and through your life. It is a joy and a blessing for me to work with her!

When I (Carrie) was first asked to consider this project, I was deeply humbled to work on something so important. The more I studied about Mary, the more I came to understand that there is much about her life and walk with God for us to learn. From the moment we asked the question, why did God choose Mary's life? the writing had become an adventure—a challenging, humbling, and sometimes difficult adventure. Mary's life brings up some important questions that we must ask ourselves. One that I have learned to continually ask is, could God come to my life today and entrust me with His great purposes?

We hope to help you clearly answer that question with a determined yes. With this book, our goal is to stay with the Scripture and see how we can apply the truths in Mary's life to our lives. It is our prayer that this book will affect your life as much as it has ours in writing it. We are praying that God will open your eyes to His will and purposes for you, and that you will see God use your life to be a blessing to others.

CHAPTER 1

PREPARED BY GOD WITH A GODLY HERITAGE

He chose us in Him before the foundation of the world, that we
should be holy and without blame before Him in love.
—EPHESIANS 1:4

IT IS VERY IMPORTANT to understand at the outset of this book that God can and will use *anyone* whose heart is fully yielded to Him. There will never be a time when God will pass over a child of His who is truly seeking to follow Him! But at times we can limit God through our perception of ourselves. Sometimes when we think about having a heritage of faith or a godly heritage, we are looking at it from a human perspective. When we are asked about our family or what type of heritage we have, we often think only of our immediate family or the people that we knew through the years. Many people, when pondering their background, naturally think about their parents and the parental relationship and influence over their lives. Some of us can look a little farther and see a loving and godly grandparent who has prayed faithfully for us. A few of us may not even know our family heritage because of extenuating circumstances. Maybe God has grafted you into another family. There are so many factors that can play a role in our heritage—but all of these things are too often limited by our human eyes.

God is not limited to our vision of the present or even the recent past! God can trace our lives all the way back to Adam. His view of heritage is far different from ours. God works in a much larger context for our life than most of us realize. What God places firmly in our heritage can often shape and influence our lives deeply. This is certainly true of Mary.

A HERITAGE OF REVIVAL

I (Henry) have often wondered why God seemed to have placed a constant burden in my life for a great revival—especially among native Indians in the nations of the United States and Canada when I was ten. Later in my life, as I meditated and stood before God, I was made aware of my heritage regarding revival and spiritual awakening. About five of my relatives on my father's side graduated from Spurgeon's college in England during a time of revival under the ministry of Charles Haddon Spurgeon. Working alongside Spurgeon and others, they did church planting across England. In addition, my uncle and aunt were missionaries in Northern China, in Harbin and Manchuria, during the great Shantung revival. This same uncle baptized me and later became my pastor during the time of God's call on my life.

God has given me a heritage that included great hearts for revival. I also think about my layman father's godly life as a businessman and a church planter. He also had a sensitive heart cry for prayer and sought for many years to see a mighty movement of God in revival.

I now see my heritage in a different context. My family's spiritual heritage was to place in me a heart cry for both church planting and revival. I led our small church in Saskatoon, Saskatchewan, in western Canada to start thirty-eight new churches. And later I was asked to direct the office of prayer, revival, and spiritual awakening for our Home Mission Board (now known as the North American Mission Board of the Southern Baptist Convention, working to reach North America for Christ), and encourage our thousands of local churches to prepare and pray for revival. I have had the privilege of being present for a number of deep touches of God in revival. On the front edge of my life, to this day, is a heart cry for revival.

Everywhere I speak, I now urge believing Christians to stand before God and let Him show them the heritage He has placed in their lives. I pray that God would reveal to them how He has pressed specific tendencies or a spiritual theme in their families. I also pray that God would show each person how to honor the Lord and know what He is doing in and through their lives. And then I encourage them to live out this revelation, this heritage, faithfully to the glory of God.

A GODLY HERITAGE

Clearly, God uses any life that is fully committed to Him, regardless of culture, upbringing, and family heritage. Everyone is responsible for his or her own choices in life, and there are many examples in Scripture where God greatly used someone who had a difficult home life and many past mistakes. There are just as many examples of people who had a nearly perfect heritage who completely missed God and His work around them. In fact, it was John the Baptist who warned the multitudes in Luke 3:8–9: "Bear fruits worthy of repentance, and do not begin to say to yourselves, 'We have Abraham as our father.' For I say to you that God is able to raise up children to Abraham from these stones."

So, although heritage is very important from God's perspective, being used by God is dependent on our obedience and love for the Lord. God's work in our lives is not limited by our background but by the decisions we make in our lives.

When we look at the heritage of having a Christian family, we look at the family members who are the most closely connected in our lives—parents, siblings, and sometimes grandparents and other close relations. Having that immediate Christian family brings specific blessings that are obvious and visible. When God begins to work in a child's life, He has a strong foundation on which to begin. Children who grow up with the love and security that should be found in the Christian home, who learn Bible verses and songs about Jesus, have a stronger foundation of belief and faith than those who have many struggles and challenges in their early years.

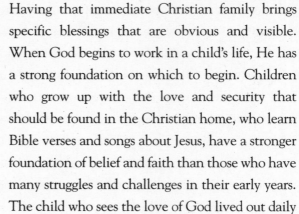

God's work in our lives is not limited by our background but by the decisions we make in our lives.

The child who sees the love of God lived out daily in the life of the family does not question God's love when he encounters the Lord. There are far fewer barriers for this child to come to the Father with an open heart. As Christian parents, it is our job to walk carefully with the Lord and to be the daily example that would lead our children to Christ.

Most of us have no knowledge of the heritage that spans the centuries. This type of godly heritage is seen most clearly in the deliberate recording of Jesus' lineage in Matthew 1:1–17 and also in Luke 3:23–38. The fact that God traces Jesus' heritage back to "Adam, the son of God" (Luke 3:38) and to Abraham (Matt. 1:1) is very significant. God wanted all people to know that from the moment of creation, He was carefully watching over the heritage of the Messiah, which would in turn mean that God was carefully watching over the heritage of Mary and Joseph as well! For God's ultimate redemptive purpose, it was important that Jesus have that traceable heritage for all to see.

This type of historical heritage has always been important to God's people to establish the link back to the blessing and promises of God. Since God had promised back in Genesis 12 to bless the seed of Abraham, it was important to be able to trace one's family heritage within the line of Abraham. The Old Testament is filled with many passages relating to the lineage of people to validate their call in life, whether it was as a king, a prophet, or another leader of God's people. Many times in Scriptures we hear not just of Abraham, but of "Abraham, Isaac, Jacob, and Joseph." The heritage of Abraham was passed on and received and lived out to the blessing of God's chosen people.

The Old Testament also places great importance on the line of David. When God chose David, He also chose all his succeeding generations. God promised that someone would always "sit on his throne." Not everyone who received this legacy from David lived it out. But Scripture mentions several who did. Second Chronicles 17:3 specifically mentions Jehoshaphat, 2 Chronicles 29:1–2 talks about the life of Hezekiah, and 2 Chronicles 34:1–2 tells us of the walk of Josiah. All are traced back to the faithfulness of King David. It is equally important to note that there are actually more kings listed from the line of David who did not follow in the godly heritage, but did evil in the sight of the Lord. Some examples are Ahaz (2 Chron. 28:1), Manasseh (2 Chron. 33:1–2), Amon (2 Chron. 33:21–22), and Jehoiakim and Jehoiachin (2 Chron. 36:5–10).

The New Testament continues to place importance on lineage. Along with the detailed account of Jesus' heritage, Zacharias's heritage is mentioned as having Abijah, a Levite priest of Nehemiah's day (Luke 1:5), and Elizabeth is of the lineage of Aaron, a significant priest in the beginning of the covenant people (also in Luke 1:5).

MARY'S HERITAGE

Mary was one who had a strong and solid foundation in her life. For her to have responded so completely with trust and faith in the Lord shows that she was well-grounded in the Scriptures at a young age. Mary's response in her "Magnificat" song in Luke 1:46–55 shows her deep understanding and training in the ways God has worked both historically and powerfully through His chosen people. (We will discuss this in greater detail in chapter 7.)

She came from the tribe of Judah and was also greatly influenced from the priestly lineage of Levi, which traditionally was always seeking to obey and fulfill the Law. It is important to understand her heritage as we seek to know how God could trust her at such a young age with the assignment of bearing the Savior of the world.

We first discover Mary's life when we read about her encounter with the angel Gabriel, who was sent by God to announce the blessing of Christ's birth (Luke 1:26–27). God, however, had been planning Mary's life and her contribution to His redemptive plan since the beginning of time. Ephesians 1:4 tell us, "He chose us in Him before the foundation of the world, that we should be holy and without blame before Him in love."

God could have chosen anyone, any place, and any time to fulfill His plan of salvation. He could have chosen to use someone who was from an honored city like Jerusalem. Jerusalem had long been the center for God's chosen people, yet the city with the great temple was passed over. At the very least, it would seem logical that God would choose someone from the region of Judea. Yet God bypassed Judea, the region of the great kings and the city of His historical blessing, and instead chose a simple girl from a simple family in Galilee. He selected the city of Nazareth, which, at that time, was seen as one of the most corrupt cities to be found in that entire region.[1] This is what prompted the statement by Nathanael in John 1:46 after hearing that Philip found the Messiah—Jesus of Nazareth: "Can anything good come out of Nazareth?"

For Nathanael, this was a valid question. The city of Nazareth, now thought to have had around fifteen thousand people, was sitting near the crossroads of two great highways. These roads were frequented by many travelers, including Roman soldiers and Greek merchants who did not carry the same values and morals as God's people.[2] Was there anything good in Nazareth? Yes! God was at work in a life that was prepared to follow Him in obedience! God is not limited by location, environment, cultural climate, or our expectations.

Mary was a simple, ordinary young woman who was chosen by God for an extraordinary moment in history. She is considered by many scholars to have been around the age of fourteen.[3] As with all girls in those days, Mary was taught the duties of a mother and homemaker from an early age. Her parents had done their best to secure her future and had betrothed her to a man named Joseph, who came from the house of David (Matt. 1:1–16). God has always linked believers together (2 Cor. 6:14). Although girls typically were not formally educated, it is clear that Mary's parents taught her about the Scriptures and her duties and responsibilities to God. Her love and obedience to the Lord were evident in her initial response to His messenger, which revealed a pattern of obedience and a heart that was pure before the Lord. In the early years of her marriage, there were also many examples of how Mary and Joseph sought to fulfill the Law, and even in Jesus' early years He was instructed in the importance of going to the temple.

Although there are not many passages relating to Mary's heritage, we can see that she was brought up in the fear and love of God by godly parents. We would like to take a look at what the Scripture does include about Mary's family, specifically her cousin Elizabeth.

OUR FAMILY'S HERITAGE

Little did I (Henry) realize that my uncle and aunt's time in China during the great Shantung revival would impact me greatly. The Shantung revival, where several hundred thousand people came to know the Lord in a personal way, deeply impacted China and many other nations of the world. This new understanding of revival would help confirm to me God's assignment in my life for revival and spiritual awakening in our day. God continues to use my family in my life.

The influence of heritage on many is well documented. I meet this regularly as I travel throughout the country speaking to different groups of people. All of my children are now actively involved in Christian ministry, and I see this surfacing in our grandchildren. The influence of their heritage on each of them is humbling to see.

Being aware of this, my wife, Marilynn, and I seek earnestly to leave a strong Christian legacy for our children. Several things in our lives seem to be evidenced in our children, whether they like it or not! The love of music, books, and missions; the love for God's people; wanting to disciple others—these are just a few things that have always been important in our lives.

I tremble to see some of our weaknesses that also influence our children. Our heritage includes both the positive and the negative.

I see many adults being careless in their influence on the next generation: obsessions with money, material things, career choices, prestige, pride, sports, etc. Most of these are not bad in and of themselves. But when these are the dominant traits in their lives, to the hindering of the will of God, misplaced priorities are seen as well in their children. Seeing this error later in life becomes a grief and burden to parents when they do not seem to be able to influence their children in the things of God. They had set their own hearts and lives in other directions, and their children followed in their paths.

GOD'S GUIDANCE

We must always take great care with our walk with the Lord, trusting in His promise to help and care for us along the way. The Bible gives us some clear direction for our lives on this aspect of how the Lord provides spiritual and even physical preparation.

The apostle Peter was so essential to the early Christian movement. After the Resurrection, Jesus stopped and took extra time with Peter, trying to prepare him for what he would face. Peter needed to have no doubt in his love for the Lord and in his assignment to feed the flock that would soon come to know the Lord. Peter's stand for his faith in Christ would be the cornerstone for the new church, and Jesus sought to prepare him for the cost that would be involved. Peter's first reaction was to compare what the Lord had told him about Peter's own future to what was in store for John. He asked, "But Lord, what about this man?" Jesus said to him, "If I will that he remain till I come, what is that to you? You follow Me" (John 21:21–22).

There is an inherent danger when we take our eyes off Jesus and begin comparing our lives to others. Did Jesus love John more than Peter? No! But they did have different assignments from the Lord.

There is an inherent danger when we take our eyes off Jesus and begin comparing our lives to others. Did Jesus love John more than Peter? No! But they did have different assignments from the Lord.

Our circumstances, environment, family life, health—none of these things should be a gauge for understanding God's love for us. Does God love some people more because He gives them a Christian home while others have a miserable family life? No! There are many examples today of women who went through very difficult experiences early in life. Yet because they allowed the Lord to help see them through it, they grew in the Lord in ways that others do not.[4] Although no one would wish for a difficult situation, some aspects of God's mercy, grace, forgiveness, and compassion can be understood no other way. If you have not had a godly heritage, look to the Lord and trust Him to use your difficult experience to bless and encourage others. A godly heritage can start with you! If you do have a godly heritage, thank the Lord for what He has given you now, and look to see how He will use that in your life and the lives of your children.

Connecting the Ordinary with the Realm of Glory
by Anne Graham Lotz

For some, an encounter with God is a quiet knowing. For others, it's more electric—as though His presence is announced by a trumpet flare, "Hail to the Chief," or flashing, strobing lights. Regardless of how He "appears," the impact is life-changing.

The first encounter with God that I can remember took place on Good Friday when I was a young girl of seven or eight years of age. I had watched Cecil B. de Mille's classic movie, *King of Kings,* on television. I vividly remember the agonizing awareness that my sin was responsible for the death of Jesus. That awareness was coupled with an overwhelming realization that He died just for me. Personally. Specifically. The encounter was so real that I whispered to God that I was sorry for my sin, and I tremblingly asked Him to forgive me. It was a life-defining, life-directing, life-determining moment. During that very first encounter, I not only became a child of God, I fell in love . . . *with Jesus.*

Within a year of that first encounter, I read the Bible through. From cover to cover. King James Version. Every verse, including the "begats." And that very first Bible reading began a journey into God's Word that continues to this day—a journey that has included a lifetime of encounters with God. Encounters that are not just daily,

but moment by moment. My encounters with God have not been . . .
mystical or ethereal,

      dreamy or visionary,

           sensational or spooky,

                spine-tingling or hair-raising.

Instead, they have been primarily an interaction with His Spirit as I have read or reflected on His Word. And they have occurred in the mundane routine of my daily life. They have come in the midst of everyday responsibilities, connecting the realm of the ordinary with the realm of glory. They have brought heaven down to me.

Like Moses encountering God in the burning bush while tending Jethro's sheep . . .

Like Jacob encountering God as he lay on the cold, hard ground, running from Esau . . .

Like Ezekiel encountering God in the midst of a storm while confined to a refugee camp . . .

Like the disciples encountering God while fishing . . .

. . . I have encountered God most frequently, not on the mountaintop of supernatural visions, but in the valley of everyday life and obedient service.

I am writing this on the plane as I return home from a trip that has included holding a *Just Give Me Jesus* revival in Kiev, Ukraine, as well as taking meetings in Moscow and St. Petersburg, Russia. Several days into this trip, worrying that my family was not well at home; suffering from what seemed to be the onset of a cold; adjusting to food, time, and cultural differences; taking unscheduled, last minute appointments; wrestling with organizers behind the scenes who tried to alter what I believed was a God-given, God-ordained program; and facing the challenge of communicating to thousands of women through an interpreter so that lives would be changed forever, I needed an "encounter" with God. So I prayed. When I opened my Bible, this verse leaped off the page, and I knew that God was speaking very distinctly and personally and specifically—to me . . . Anne, *"My God shall supply all your needs according to His riches in glory by Christ Jesus."* There was no doubt. I knew I had encountered Him . . . *again.*

Much like her father, Anne Graham Lotz is one of the premier speakers within the Christian community today. Yet she would be the first to tell you she is just an ordinary person. It is her deep relationship with the Lord that makes her life extraordinary! Although she had a wonderful and godly heritage, her relationship with the Lord was a personal choice she made at a young age. She chose to serve and follow Him, even when there was a cost involved. Many times I (Henry) have been a speaker at the same conferences with Anne, and I have carefully watched God express His grace and love through her words. She is a strong communicator, but it is the life and testimony behind her words that make them powerful.

A HERITAGE OF COMMITMENT

"You are so lucky to have a family like yours!" I (Carrie) hear this statement all the time. When I was younger I would just smile, nod my head politely, and wonder if they knew the same family I did! I always thought the statement was curious because we were just an ordinary family like everyone else. As I grew, I saw that we were different.

In my teenage years I realized that I was one of the few whose parents were still together. I watched as many of my friends struggled through their parents' divorce, and they told me that it was only a matter of time before my parents divorced as well. Yet deep in my heart I knew that my parents would never divorce. Their love for the Lord and their love and commitment to each other could not be broken.

Because most of my friends did not have a relationship with the Lord, they thought I was just being naive as they once were. After all, their parents had loved each other as well, but it still wasn't enough to keep their family together. Commitment cannot last a lifetime. I could not help them understand that it was my parents' commitment and obedience to the Lord, their desire to always please Him, which would keep their marriage vows from ever being broken. They would never break a vow they made before the Lord. This gave me a security in my developmental years that most of my friends never had.

I now have a new understanding of the statement "You are so lucky to have a family like yours," and it has taken on a deeper meaning for me. My family taught me to be committed to God's truths and His ways and is teaching me through their example how to be like Christ.

How did my parents learn to do this? They learned by searching the Scriptures and applying everything to their lives and to the life of our family. But along with this, both my parents were blessed with solid Christian families and parents who also searched the Scriptures and sought to obey the Lord. God began to connect some things in my heart. When I spoke to my father about this, he broadened my perspective even further on the Christian heritage on his family's side. My mother's parents served the Lord faithfully throughout their lives and were missionaries to Africa in their retirement years. My mother's sister and brother have also served overseas, impacting God's work throughout Europe and Singapore.

There is something very special about a godly heritage. It is close to the heart of God to raise children in the faith and train them in His ways and truths. Scripture records several examples of people whom God called and chose at a very young age, often because of their early training in God's ways. But as we said in the beginning, God can and will use *anyone* whose heart is prepared to be obedient to His call regardless of personal or family background. If you did not have a godly Christian family and you found the Lord's mercy later in life, know that the godly heritage can begin with you and your family.

If you did not have a godly Christian family and you found the Lord's mercy later in life, know that the godly heritage can begin with you and your family.

Remember that God is not limited to our vision of the present or even the recent past! Just because we don't know all that God has placed within our heritage doesn't mean it's not there. Never become discouraged thinking that your life is not special and precious in the sight of the Lord. He planned *your* life from the foundation of the world.

Also know that if you are a believer in Christ and have a relationship with Him as your Savior, you are a child of the King! Through Jesus you have a rich heritage that cannot be taken away from you.

The Bible is the record of God's eternal purposes. From Genesis to Revelation, God unfolds His heart in the midst of the real world as He chooses people through whom He will work. God always takes the initiative with each of us individually, or with a group of people like Israel.

Because He is God, His ways most often surprise those He chooses and calls. He often seems to drop into our everyday lives, giving us an opportunity to be a part of His work. There doesn't have to be a "big event" for God to speak to us. God has always, however, required faith, because without faith it is impossible to please God (Heb. 11:6). So God reads our hearts and looks at our character to see if He can trust us with eternal matters. To God, there is too much at stake to trust eternity to those of us who are unwilling to yield every part of our lives to Him. Choose to be one to whom God can entrust eternal matters!

In the beginning was the Word, and the Word was with God, and the Word was God. He was in the beginning with God. All things were made through Him, and without Him nothing was made that was made. In Him was life, and the life was the light of men. (John 1:1–4)

When God chooses to encounter us, He already knows the condition of our hearts. When God allows us to experience Him in a personal way, it is because He already has a plan in motion, and He wants to use us. That moment of His encounter is not the time to decide if we have the faith to respond in obedience. That decision must be made *before* God calls. We then will answer Him with "Yes, Lord." When God sees our heart that is prepared to obey Him, then He will reveal Himself and His plan. Has His Lordship been settled in your life? Then be prepared to see Him at work through you!

Our responsibility is to make sure that our heart is always prepared and pure before the Lord. A wholly yielded life, like Mary's, is what God is looking for. We will continue to discuss throughout this book what it means to have a pure heart that God can use.

QUESTIONS FOR STUDY AND RESPONSE

1. Mary had been blessed with a mighty heritage and was raised with a love for God and His laws. This made an enormous impact on her life, preparing her heart to serve the Lord. Has God blessed you with a godly family? If not, can you commit to beginning a Christian heritage with your children and conscientiously choosing to raise them in God's truths?

2. Do you know about the heritage you have in the Lord? If you have sometimes felt like a spiritual orphan, take some time to look through Jesus' history and heritage. For if you are a child of the King, you have a mighty spiritual heritage indeed!

3. When God came to Mary's life, He already knew her heart, her love, and her obedient spirit. Just like Mary, God knows us today and has an incredible purpose and plan for our lives. How has God been preparing your life to serve His purposes? Have you told your children of those moments in your life that God encountered you?

4. Proverbs 22:1 tells us that a good name is to be chosen rather than riches. What have you placed as a priority in your life? Have "riches" been more important to you than securing a good name for the future of your children and grandchildren?

CHAPTER 2

How God Can Work Through a Family

A good name is to be chosen rather than great riches . . .
—Proverbs 22:1

I (Carrie) must admit that I've taken a great deal of teasing in my life with four older brothers. God decided that early in my life I needed some toughening up to be able to stand firm—and my brothers provided me with a lot of practice. I watched as the brothers would sometimes tease and give one another a hard time, yet when there was a common foe on the block or at school, the bonds that united them could not be broken, and no one could take them on. They had a unique way of communicating and a loyalty to each other when the going got tough.

This continued as we grew older; God worked individually in each of our lives, calling us into a lifetime of His service. We have many of the same bedrock foundation beliefs, yet our callings are all completely unique. We have all decided to follow the Lord regardless of what He asks or where He decides to put us.

God builds something rare into the family relationship. Being the youngest, it is often easier to watch the others in different situations, gauging their actions and reactions. It was interesting to watch the response when my two oldest brothers felt led of the Lord to work together in a church. To me it was no surprise. They had always worked well together and seemed to be able to work through any problems. Others, however, were quite shocked and had predictions of doom for their relationship and the church. Needless to say, they did work well together. The church grew in number and in spirit until the Lord led one to become the president of the Canadian Southern Baptist Seminary in Cochrane, Alberta.

While my husband, Wendell, and I were in Canada, we taught at the Canadian seminary as the missionaries in residence. We also were involved at Bow Valley Baptist Church where my third brother is the pastor. People started to tease me about having one brother for a "boss" and another as my "spiritual leader." Then they realized I loved it! It was a joy to see all that the Lord was doing in and through their lives, knowing that I could go to them with anything, and they would take the time to help me through it.

GOD'S USE OF FAMILIES

There are many examples throughout the Scripture of God using families as a tool for His purposes. God clearly worked through the bloodline of Abraham, giving a special blessing to His people throughout the generations that followed. The New Testament also has strong examples of the importance of family. Jesus Himself chose two sets of brothers as His first called disciples: Andrew and Peter, and James and John (Matt. 4:18–22).

It is also interesting that John the Baptist, the forerunner to the Savior, was actually related to Him! The gospel of Luke tells the testimony of Elizabeth and Zacharias's journey, and Matthew tells of John's impact on the people and of his desire to help God's people return to Him. His message of "Repent, for the kingdom of heaven is at hand!"

(Matt. 3:2) prepared people's hearts to look for the Messiah. Indeed, John was the one the Father chose to herald Christ's earthly ministry as John baptized Jesus with water.

Why are we taking so much time to study Mary's relatives? Of all the details that could have been included about her life and the life of her family, the Scripture records only the story of her cousin, Elizabeth, with her husband, Zacharias. This couple made such an impact on Mary's young life that many years later Luke would include it in his Gospel's birth story of Jesus. We would like to take some time to search through the truths of the importance of family because it played an important role for Mary. Her cousin greatly influenced and encouraged her as she started out her journey as the mother of Jesus. Mary was young and alone. She had received a significant revelation from the Lord but needed someone in her life to give her perspective. Elizabeth was that person in Mary's life.

Always keep in mind that the faithfulness of a family can begin through you! God does not play favorites; He looks for obedience. The Pharisees of Jesus' day had impeccable bloodlines, yet they not only missed the time of Christ's coming, they killed Him! Every Christian, regardless of his or her heritage, is only one decision away from being used by God through personal obedience or from being at a spiritual standstill by choosing disobedience.

Always keep in mind that the faithfulness of a family can begin through you! God does not play favorites; He looks for obedience. The Pharisees of Jesus' day had impeccable bloodlines, yet they not only missed the time of Christ's coming, they killed Him!

ELIZABETH AND ZACHARIAS
(LUKE 1:5–25, 39–45)

Elizabeth and Zacharias's testimony gives us a unique insight into the lineage of Mary and how God can use the family to encourage and instruct us in our faith. The Scripture in Luke gives us details of the angel Gabriel's conversation with Mary.

> "Now indeed, Elizabeth your relative has also conceived a son in her old age; and this is now the sixth month for her who was called barren. For with God nothing will be impossible." Then Mary said, "Behold the maidservant of the Lord! Let it be to me according to your word." And the angel departed from her. Now Mary arose in those days and went into the hill country with haste, to a city of Judah, and entered the house of Zacharias and greeted Elizabeth. (Luke 1:36–40)

Elizabeth's life began with so much promise. She was blessed with a very godly heritage, and her family was from the priestly line of Moses' brother Aaron (Luke 1:5). Her given name, meaning "one who swears by God" was also the name of Aaron's wife (Exod. 6:23).[1] This fact shows she was raised knowing the priestly heritage and that it was important to her family as well. She was betrothed to Zacharias, a man from another line of priests whose name means "Jehovah Remembers."[2] It is extremely likely that this marriage contract was seen as a wonderful blessing from the Lord. Although it was not required for a priest to marry a woman within the priestly heritage, it was seen as a special blessing.[3] From both the Jewish society and their families' perspective, great things were in the future of this godly couple. Yet God's ways are not our ways, and the blessing did not take the form that the people of their day expected. God's blessings rarely do!

In the time of Elizabeth and Zacharias, people believed that the blessing of the Lord could be easily measured in society by many outward signs. Some of the visible signs that God was truly blessing one's life and one's family included bearing many children, having good land with plenty of stock, and having good health and an abundance of wealth. In addition, in the case of a priest like Zacharias, he would have been chosen by God to represent the people before Him in the temple. These were all visible signs that God was truly blessing one's life and family. The most important of these were the blessing of children and being chosen to stand before God in the temple.

This celebrated union began with such promise. Yet as Elizabeth and Zacharias went through their marriage, there was rising concern as they remained childless. This couple, who had so much potential, was progressing through life without a child. This was a particular humiliation for Elizabeth, as the chief function of the woman in the marriage was to bear children—especially sons.[4] This was a source of deep heartache, as we later see her reaction to the blessing of motherhood. Luke 1:24–25 records her response: "Now after those days his wife Elizabeth conceived; and she hid herself five months, saying, 'Thus the Lord has dealt with me, in the days when he looked on me, to take away my reproach among people.'"

There is a very similar heart cry recorded in the Old Testament. The first chapter of 1 Samuel tells us the story of Hannah who, although she experienced great love from her husband, faced a great deal of ridicule and misery for not conceiving a child. Verses 6–7 tell us: "And her rival [her husband's other wife, Peninnah] also provoked her severely, to make her miserable, because the LORD had closed her womb. So it was, year by year, when she went up to the house of the LORD, that she provoked her; therefore she [Hannah] wept and did not eat."

Later, while Hannah was crying out to the Lord, she talked about her "affliction" and how discouraged she was. In a society that figured a woman's worth by the number of children she had, to be barren would have been a very difficult burden for any woman. It was seen as a specific punishment that only the Lord could give. Both Hannah's and Elizabeth's struggle clearly shows how difficult their lives had been under the label "barren."

PASSED OVER . . . AGAIN

To make matters worse, Zacharias was continually passed over, never chosen by the casting of lots to represent the people before the Lord. We know that Zacharias was "well advanced in years" (Luke 1:7). He had been prepared all his life for the one moment when he would represent the people and come before the Lord on their behalf. Because this was such a coveted duty for a priest, they were only given the opportunity once in a lifetime. Since there were many priests in this time period, they were divided up into twenty-four divisions, with six family clans in each division.[5] So every twenty-four weeks Zacharias made the journey to the temple, wondering each time if the Lord would allow the casting of lots to fall on him. Each time he was passed by. As those who were chosen were taken out of the circle, Zacharias would have felt the isolation and embarrassment of continually being rejected. Although there may have been others who had also not been chosen, it is unlikely that they would also have been childless.[6]

Culturally speaking, this couple did not seem to be pleasing to the Lord because He clearly was not visibly blessing them. Society would have believed that, although this couple may have appeared faithful, they were certainly being punished by the Lord for some sin in their life.

> **A good name is better than precious ointment.**
> **(Eccles. 7:1)**

Yet nothing could be further from the truth! Not only was God pleased with them, but He was about to use their lives for one of the greatest events in history—an event that would be dramatically connected with the coming of the promised Savior!

GOD ENTRUSTED THEM

Although Elizabeth and Zacharias most likely faced persecution and ridicule from their peers, the Bible consistently mentions the continued righteousness of both before God. Luke 1:6 goes as far to say that "they were both righteous before God, walking in all the commandments and ordinances of the Lord *blameless*" (emphasis added)!

Zacharias and Elizabeth did not just endure this difficulty; they remained dedicated and obedient to the Lord. It is because of this obedience and steadfastness that God could entrust the life of John the Baptist into their care, knowing that they would teach him all the things of God. Jesus Himself said, "Among those born of women there has not risen one greater than John the Baptist" (Matt. 11:11).

One of the two who heard John speak, and followed him, was Andrew, Simon Peter's brother. He first found his own brother Simon, and said to him, "We have found the Messiah" (which is translated, the Christ). And he brought him to Jesus. Now when Jesus looked at him, He said, "You are Simon the son of Jonah. You shall be called Cephas" (which is translated, A Stone). (John 1:40–42)

John's life was so important as a predecessor to Christ that it had to be entrusted to a couple who had chosen to believe God throughout their lives, who struggled through adversity and pain and yet still remained faithful.[7]

Often we want a great assignment, but we don't realize the cost that comes with it. Elizabeth and Zacharias had years of disappointment and grief, but through these experiences they were able to be used to impact God's Kingdom, as well as instruct and encourage Mary as she was about to fulfill God's plan for her life.

Clearly, God's ways are not our ways. To the people around Elizabeth and Zacharias, it seemed that God had chosen not to bless this couple because they were unworthy. Yet God had chosen and prepared them to announce the coming of salvation to Israel! What a difference! God used this incredible example of Elizabeth in Mary's life in a very special way. The Father had been working, bringing everything together in His fullness of time. He had prepared everything in advance, working through every situation, to further His plan for salvation. When the time came to reveal His plan to Mary, His servant, He used the life of her faithful older cousin, Elizabeth. Although we don't know the depth of their relationship, we are told that Mary made "haste" to visit her cousin and confirm all that was revealed to her. Luke 1:39–40 tells us that after the angel revealed God's plan for Mary, she "arose in those days and went into the hill country with haste, to a city of Judah, and entered the house of Zacharias and greeted Elizabeth."

With Elizabeth having had her own experience with the Lord, Mary was able to have that needed confirmation and affirmation that could only have come from her cousin. Mary knew of the difficulties Elizabeth had faced and probably respected her a great deal. Their first encounter was exactly what Mary's heart would have needed, knowing what she was about to face in the coming months. Living as an unwed mother in her society, she would have faced untold rejection, gossip, and ridicule and might have already been disowned by her immediate family, whom the Scripture never mentions. Mary received the encouragement and strength that she needed from Elizabeth.

> And it happened, when Elizabeth heard the greeting of Mary, that the babe leaped in her womb; and Elizabeth was filled with the Holy Spirit. Then she spoke out with a loud voice and said, "Blessed are you among women, and blessed is the fruit of your womb! But why is this granted to me, that the mother of my Lord should come to me? For indeed, as soon as the voice of your greeting sounded in my ears, the babe leaped in my womb for joy. Blessed is she who believed, for there will be a fulfillment of those things which were told her from the Lord." (Luke 1:41–45)

Elizabeth, filled with the Holy Spirit, was able to bring the words that Mary needed to hear. She was able to reassure this young girl that she was not alone and that others recognized the favor that God had bestowed upon her. The three months that she spent with this family changed Mary's life, giving her perspective to follow God's will for her life and the life of her Son, Jesus.

This godly couple was a part of Mary's family. God did not haphazardly place Mary within this family or in this period in time. God does not miss details! He knew the plans He had for Mary; He knew what she would need to be successful and obedient to the call. He knew what kind of love, support, and encouragement she would need. He also knew that Mary needed the family support and teaching that this tried and true couple would provide.

What an exciting and humbling realization it is when we understand that God does the exact same thing in our lives today. We may tend to think that God has forgotten about a situation or that He isn't showing as much favor to us as others. But just as we are all uniquely created, so is our assignment and call from the Lord. And so is the affirmation God grants us through family and friends.

Trusting the Lord in All Things
by Jan Robertson

My husband and I had been married for about two years when I went to my doctor for a routine physical exam. After the examination my doctor asked me when my husband and I planned to start our family. He advised that due to my medical problems, it would probably be difficult for me to conceive and that I shouldn't wait too long before trying to have children.

For the next nine years I endured three surgeries and numerous procedures designed to help me become pregnant. None were successful. During those nine years, I always remained hopeful that eventually I would conceive. Toward the end of that time, however, I became very discouraged. I didn't want to go through any more medical procedures. I was tired of the struggle and began to lose hope of ever knowing the joy of being a mother. When my sister-in-law became pregnant with her third child, I cried. I didn't want to congratulate her; I didn't even want to talk with her. It just seemed so unfair that I didn't have one child and she was about to have her third.

Soon after that time, my husband and I were chaperoning a group of teenagers from our church who were attending a camp on the banks of the Satilla River in South Georgia. One morning before daylight, I eased out of camp and went to sit on the dock. I was surrounded by a gray haze that covered the river and crept up to surround me. That was the perfect setting for my mood. I must have sat there for an hour, praying and crying out to God. I just couldn't understand why He would not bless us with children. Even though He had comforted me with many promises through Scripture over the past years, I was not very happy with His timing. So, that morning, I sat and cried; I begged; I pleaded; I asked why; I asked when . . .

In the midst of my ranting, I was suddenly quieted by the sound of His voice. He said so clearly: "*Be still and know that I am God!*" He stopped me in my tracks. I have never had so powerful a word from the Lord. He was definitely my Abba, my Father. The message was clear. "Be still, child! Don't you trust Me? Haven't I promised that you would have children?" I felt an immediate peace and sense of anticipation of God's plans for our family. I never again questioned that we would be parents, and I began to watch for His plan.

A few months later, my husband and I were approached about the possibility of adopting a little boy. He was going to be taken from his teenage mother and placed in foster care because he was being neglected and possibly abused. The birth mother decided that she would give him up for adoption to a Christian couple, and she had asked our friend to help her find the right couple. We had never considered the option of adoption, but when confronted with this situation, my husband and I went to the Lord and asked Him was this His provision for us? After much prayer, we told them that we would gladly take the little boy. We waited for a call from the lawyer who would handle the adoption, but it never came. The birth mother had changed her mind and had basically disappeared.

Even though our hearts were broken, this incident helped us realize that we really wanted to pursue adoption. We asked God to guide us as we began this journey. We began to inquire of adoption agencies, and we also made everyone around aware that we wanted to adopt. We wrote letters to every doctor, lawyer, and pastor that we knew. Four months later, the call came that eventually led to the adoption of our daughter, Christy. Never has there been a more welcomed child. The joy that she has brought to us and our families is beyond expression.

One day I was thinking back to the day that we were first approached about adopting the little boy. That was the catalyst that led us to pursue adoption. I looked at a calendar and realized that from that date until the day Christy was born was exactly nine months! How exciting to realize that from the moment she was conceived, God planned for us to be her mother and father.

Christy loved dolls from the first year of her life. Her dolls always had personality and were members of our family. When she was two years old, God answered the prayer that she prayed every night: "God, please send me a *real live* baby." Christy's little sister, Meg, came to us in a similarly miraculous way, leaving absolutely no doubt that God had chosen her for us and our family for her.

God's ways are not our ways, and I'm so thankful! His plan for our family far surpassed all that we could have asked.

Jan, along with her husband, Dan, have been true friends to our family through the years. After Jan spent several years as a schoolteacher, the Lord directly linked her with our family to help transcribe tapes of Henry's sermons and be a part of the editing process for many different projects (including this one!). Her giving spirit, faithful prayers, and listening ear have always been such an encouragement. Jan currently owns a workout gym for women and continues to share and make an impact on all the people God brings into her life.

EVERYONE WAS "FAIR GAME"

One of the more influential people in my (Henry) teenage life was my grandmother Boucher, my mother's mother. She was a wise and godly woman who was widowed through all the years that I knew her. Her home was always pleasant, and the walls were filled with Scripture passages. It was very important to her that there were Scriptures in every room in her house. She was a great witness to her neighbors and community, and no one was exempt from a kind word that directed others to Christ. The milkman, the mailman, the bread man, and the meter man; all who came to her door were "fair game" and were therefore told of the great love of her Lord!

She was a pillar in her church, always sitting in her spot so that others would always know where to come when they wanted to talk. She continually testified in prayer meetings to God's goodness to her and never uttered a critical or negative word about others. When I was a teenager we moved to the same city. I remember with great clarity how she would put her arm around my shoulders and encourage and exhort me to take care in my walk with the Lord and to always be faithful to Him. What an impact she made in my life! Is it any wonder that all of her children and all of her grandchildren are Christians, and all admired her greatly? To the best of my knowledge, she continually served the Lord throughout her days.

We will never know of all the ways our lives will influence others. Our influence on others may come from one specific moment in time when a kind word will make a difference in someone's life, or from a continued mentorship of one with whom we've chosen to work. In particular, we often have no idea how we have influenced those in our own family.

Elizabeth and Zacharias had no way of knowing that, because of their situation and all the difficulties faced together, they would play such an important role in God's plan of redemption. Would all that pain and suffering through the years have been worth it to them, knowing that God had been preparing them for His purposes? Those whose lives have been chosen to impact God's kingdom would say yes! This couple was tested by fire and came through with God's blessing and validation of their lives for all the people to see. Every moment in their lives would be weighed against being an integral part of God's redemptive plan. Their lives would now include great joy.

> You will have joy and gladness, and many will rejoice at his birth. For he will be great in the sight of the Lord, and shall drink neither wine nor strong drink. He will also be filled with the Holy Spirit, even from his mother's womb. And he will turn many of the children of Israel to the Lord their God. (Luke 1:14–16)

There are also many "hidden" difficulties in our society today that women face. One of the most stressful can be the inability to have children. Most women secretly wonder if this miracle will happen for them at some point in their lives.

I (Carrie) remember when I was told that because of all the chemo and radiation therapy I endured with my cancer treatments there was no way to tell whether I would be able to have children. Initially at sixteen, I did not know how that would affect my life. At the time I was just happy that I had survived and was unconcerned about the details or future repercussions of my illness.

Later in life, however, I was concerned that it would affect my future marriage. Would a future husband be okay with the possibility of not having children? Before my husband and I became serious about a relationship,

I told him my concerns and wanted to be upfront with any issues that we might face later. Thankfully, this was not difficult for him! He knew that God had put us together and was completely unfazed by what I had thought could be a problem. This was the first of many instances to come when I realized that men and women have completely different perspectives on many things!

We found out we were able to have children when I became pregnant with Elizabeth, our first child. About three years later, Joshua was born on the mission field in Germany. God did not have to grant us these blessings, but we are so thankful for the family He entrusted to us.

There are still some societal pressures today to have children. Parents pressure you to make them grandparents, or friends with children feel sure you need to experience having children as well. Society sometimes judges a person without children as incomplete. Although there is often no slight intended, it can bring about feelings of inadequacy and depression. But through Christ, those without children can know great peace in the understanding that God can turn any difficulty or seeming tragedy into a beautiful and incomparable purpose. Only God can bring perspective on the challenges we face. If we allow Him to work in our lives, He can turn any seeming difficulty or setback into a victory for our lives. Often we can even come to realize that what we saw as a setback or struggle was actually God preparing our lives for the greatest blessing that we could experience.

The unconditional relationship within the family is something to be cherished. When you see God working in your family, whether it is a big or small event, seek to understand what God is doing and if there is something of which you need to be a part. Even if your family members are not believers in Christ, you know that He is always working around you to draw others to Himself. Little things every day allow you to help bring light and hope and peace to another loved one or friend. Whether or not you come from a Christian family, God placed you in your family for a particular purpose. Maybe He placed you there not for how they can help you grow, but so that you can be that blessing to your family that He knew *they* needed.

QUESTIONS FOR STUDY AND RESPONSE

1. What kind of family has God placed you in? Have you looked at your family from God's perspective, seeing His activity in their lives and looking for ways you can encourage, support, and bless them?

2. Without question, Elizabeth and Zacharias would have been faithful to the Lord regardless of whether they ever had children. They were already "well advanced in years" and didn't have any reason to expect that their childlessness would change. Have you dealt with the struggle of not having children? Have you allowed it to put a barrier between you and your Lord? If so, ask God to forgive you and heal your relationship with Him, giving you His perspective on how your life can be a blessing to others.

3. Elizabeth and Zacharias went through years of suffering and pain, not knowing why God was "withholding" His blessing from them. It wasn't until much later in life that, because of their blameless walk before the Lord, He poured out His blessing and honored them with John the Baptist. Are you willing to wait through discouragement and pain to see how God can use this in your life for His purposes? Is your life ready for the "big assignments"?

4. Sometimes it may seem that our lives are being passed over or forgotten as opportunities arise. Are you willing to remain faithful to the Lord amidst your disappointments and wait to see how He will use them in your life?

5. Elizabeth and Zacharias had both experienced great pain and discouragement in their lives. God often uses times of great discouragement and disappointment to strengthen our relationship with Him and encourage others in their faith. Have there been times of great pain and difficulty in your life? Have they strengthened your walk with the Lord? Have you allowed those times to be an encouragement to others?

6. Like God did for Mary, God has placed people of great encouragement in our lives. Mary needed Elizabeth and Zacharias's encouragement and teaching through this very important time. God has also provided special people to help us walk through the difficult times and who help us keep a perspective when we cannot see beyond the situation. Who are the people God has given you who have helped in your walk with Him? If you can't think of anyone, ask God to show you who He's provided.

CHAPTER 3

How God Can Use a Marriage

Do not be unequally yoked together with unbelievers. For what fellowship has righteousness with lawlessness? And what communion has light with darkness? And what accord has Christ with Belial? Or what part has a believer with an unbeliever? And what agreement has the temple of God with idols? For you are the temple of the living God. As God has said: "I will dwell in them and walk among them. I will be their God, and they shall be My people."
—2 CORINTHIANS 6:14–16

WHEN WE TALK ABOUT MARRIAGE, it is essential to see what God intended the marriage commitment to be. There can be no greater influence on a person's life or future than who the person chooses to marry. This was true for Mary's life as she sought to understand and obey all that God had revealed to her. She needed a life partner who would understand and support her and who wouldn't ridicule or belittle her experience with the Lord. Although she was highly favored and had strong character and faith, God knew that she would need the support system that comes within a strong marriage partnership.

BETROTHAL IN NEW TESTAMENT TIMES

Many significant facts about the traditional Jewish betrothal and marriage ceremony are valuable for us to understand Mary and her life with Joseph. Typically, a girl was betrothed between twelve and thirteen years of age, but the betrothal could occur earlier. The man would have been older than the girl due to the understanding that he should be able to support a family, so he would have had to be somewhat established in a trade. Usually, marriages took place within tribes and typically between relatives, such as cousins or even uncle to niece. Both Mary and Joseph were from the tribe of Judah and descended from David.

The betrothal was performed in a ceremony in the presence of witnesses. This ceremony itself was usually simple and was often followed by a meal. The betrothal contract could be compared to a prenuptial agreement today and was legally binding to both people. The marriage contract was presented at the betrothal, and it specified what the father of the bride must pay and how much reverted back to the wife in the event of a divorce or the death of the husband. The groom also gave a gift to the bride at this time.

Who can find a virtuous wife? For her worth is far above rubies. The heart of her husband safely trusts her; so he will have no lack of gain. She does him good and not evil all the days of her life. (Prov. 31:10–12)

The bride was called his wife, and she would be considered a widow if the groom died. She could also be divorced, and she could be stoned to death as the penalty for adultery. The marriage ceremony could take place up to a year after the betrothal.

On the eve of the marriage ceremony, the bride would leave her family and make her way to her bridegroom's house. She was usually accompanied by her companions. As she came to her groom's house, the couple would be crowned with garlands, and the legal marriage contract signed.[1]

CARRIE'S MARRIAGE DREAMS

Like most girls, I had dreams and plans of who I would marry some day. My perspective on marriage, of course, came from my own experience within my family—and I knew I wanted the same type of deep commitment that my parents shared. I was disappointed when I was not married as I graduated from university—which had been my childhood plan! But I knew that I would meet the "perfect" man in God's timing. It's just that God's timing was not my timing. My family liked to joke that God had to take extra time preparing some poor soul for me!

God's plan was for me to stay on the course He set for my life. I knew that God had called my life into mission service, and I needed to prepare as best I could so that God would not be limited with my options. I continued to seminary and began preparing to enter the ministry—even if I entered it alone. As I was faithful to what God revealed to me, God brought Wendell into my life in my final semester in seminary.

I am so thankful that God allowed me the extra time to prepare my heart and life for what we would undertake in the future. My studies have proved just as essential as my husband's studies, and both have helped us greatly on the mission field. Although I was ready to be married out of college, God knew that I needed to be prepared spiritually to face the challenges ahead.

God also needed to make sure that I was the wife that Wendell needed to complete God's call on his life. We have faced many different challenges and difficulties living overseas, immersed in another language and culture. I'm so thankful that the Lord took the needed time to secure and prepare our marriage to stand firm!

THE HUSBAND AND WIFE RELATIONSHIP

When looking at the background of Mary's life, it is essential that we also look at the life partner that God gave to her. Mary's marriage to Joseph had a significant impact on her life. This is what God purposed for marriage in the beginning. "Now the Lord God said, 'It is not good (sufficient, satisfactory) that the man should be alone; I will make him a helper meet (suitable, adapted, complementary) for him'" (Gen. 2:18 AMP). Then God brought Eve to Adam, and they began the human race, having children as God commanded them when He said, "Be fruitful and multiply" (Gen. 1:28).

From Genesis and creation to the very moment God announced to Mary, "Behold, you will conceive in your womb and bring forth a Son, and shall call His name Jesus" (Luke 1:31), couples brought forth children. This was always a sign of God's favor on them, especially if the first-born was a son.

God had already prepared a husband for Mary who would match everything she would face. Joseph was a godly man, as he was described in Matthew 1:19: "Joseph her husband, being a just man [an upright man] . . ." He would be for Mary a provider and protector, and he would be a guide and spiritual leader for her and the family. The family would be what God had purposed from the beginning. He was Mary's equal in every way: both had a godly heritage, both were seen as spiritually upright, and both had a heart set on obedience and sought to follow God's laws. God, who chose Mary to be the mother of Jesus before the foundation of the world, also chose Joseph as His earthly father and teacher.

What we know about Joseph from Scripture gives us justification for sensing he was brought up and guided in his religious culture. History sheds some light on Joseph's background in a general sense. History shows us how children, especially boys, were viewed by the culture. Rabbi Jehudah, one of the writers of the Mishnah (Jewish law), maps out the stages of life for a boy in the Mishnah:

At 5 years of age—reading the Scriptures
At 10—learning the Mishnah
At 13—bound to the commandments
At 15—study of the Talmud (ancient Jewish writings that make up the basis for Jewish law)
At 18—marriage
At 20—pursuit of a trade
At 30—full of vigor
At 40—maturity of reason
At 50—for counsel
At 60—commencement of agedness
At 70—grey age
At 80—advanced old age[2]

This chart gives us a cultural glimpse of how Joseph and Jesus grew up. They were grounded in the Scriptures from an early age. Around the age of five when children began learning and reading Scripture, their education became the responsibility of the father. The synagogue assisted the father in this instruction. Joseph and Jesus probably made regular trips to the synagogue for these lessons in Scripture and law.

The first thing a Jewish child would be taught is the Shema, from Deuteronomy 6:4–5, "Hear, O Israel: The LORD our God, the LORD is one! You shall love the LORD your God with all your heart, with all your soul, and with all your strength."³ This command is the foundation of the relationship with God. Further in this passage God admonishes parents: "You shall teach them diligently to your children" (v. 7).

> **And these words which I command you today shall be in your heart. You shall teach them diligently to your children, and shall talk of them when you sit in your house, when you walk by the way, when you lie down, and when you rise up. You shall bind them as a sign on your hand, and they shall be as frontlets between your eyes. You shall write them on the doorposts of your house and on your gates. (Deut. 6:6–9)**

Jesus learned these lessons well. Matthew records His temptation in the desert, where Jesus used Deuteronomy 6:13 as His defense. Deuteronomy 6 would have been one of the first lessons learned by Jesus from His father, Joseph. About twenty-five years later, this lesson would serve to defend Him against the temptation of Satan.

Joseph was a good provider. He was a carpenter, earning a good living and having a good reputation. They were not wealthy but were able to support a growing family. As Joseph taught Jesus about Scripture and law, he also would have taught Him carpentry. The firstborn boy was expected to follow in his father's footsteps, and Joseph would have spent many hours with Jesus teaching Him.⁴ The people living in Jesus' home region knew of Jesus through His trade, commenting, "Is this not the carpenter, the son of Mary . . . ?" (Mark 6:3).

As the spiritual leader in their home, Joseph walked faithfully with God. Mary may have told Joseph of her encounter with Gabriel, an angel of God who stood in His presence and brought God's message of His salvation through her Son, Jesus (Luke 1:26–28). It is obvious he believed, out of his own personal walk with God. For when an angel came to him from God, he received God's clear message to him not to put Mary away but to receive God's favor to Mary and then to him also (Matt. 1:19–25). His response to God's encounter with him in a dream was immediate obedience:

> But while he thought about these things, behold, an angel of the Lord appeared to him in a dream, saying, "Joseph, son of David, do not be afraid to take to you Mary your wife, for that which is conceived in her is of the Holy Spirit. And she will bring forth a Son, and you shall call his name JESUS, for He will save His people from their sins." . . . Then Joseph, being aroused from sleep, did as the angel of the Lord commanded him and took to him his wife, and did not know her [she remained a virgin] till she had brought forth her firstborn Son. And he called His name JESUS. (Matt. 1:20–21, 24–25)

As a husband and spiritual leader in his family, he was also their protector. When the angel again warned him of Herod's plan to kill his Son and said that they must flee immediately into Egypt until it was safe to return, Joseph obeyed quickly (Matt. 2:13–14). Joseph remained close to God, and the Lord continued to alert him as to how to be the protector of his family. It was only when the angel announced that it was safe to return from Egypt that he guided his family back home (Matt. 2:19–23).

Joseph made provision and protection available to his family. He also was a spiritual pacesetter in keeping the Law. He kept the Law for the rituals and feasts and honored the Lord with sacrifices—even if they were the smaller sacrifices of those who were poor (Luke 2:22–24). His lack of wealth did not interfere with his obedience to the Law. (We will discuss the specifics of Joseph and Mary's obedience in chapter 9.)

Joseph also guided his family as they "went to Jerusalem every year at the Feast of the Passover" (Luke 2:41). By the time Jesus was twelve years old, He had been greatly influenced by His parents as they kept the Law faithfully. This family influence was remarkable in its effect on the obedience of Jesus in His life and ministry. He, too, lived consistently according to the Scriptures as He had been taught.

MARY AS A WIFE

Mary, as Joseph's wife and mother of his children, also contributed greatly to their home. From the beginning, God had a great role for her as He had with Joseph. She supported the spiritual leadership and decisions of Joseph and was a strong, faithful homemaker and teacher of the children. They both took seriously the instruction of God to teach their children:

> Hear, O Israel: The LORD our God, the LORD is one! You shall love the LORD your God with all your heart, with all your soul, and with all your strength. And these words which I command you today shall be in your heart. You shall teach them diligently to your children, and shall talk of them when you sit in your house, when you walk by the way, when you lie down, and when you rise up. You shall bind them as a sign on your hand, and they shall be as frontlets between your eyes. You shall write them on the doorposts of your house and on your gates. (Deut. 6:4–9)

Both Joseph and Mary knew the Law and sought to keep God's commands before their family—as the Scripture instructs. Not only did Joseph and Mary individually have significant influence in the family, but they shaped their family together. Both needed to "hear from God" and obey together. Both Mary and Joseph heard from an angel of God when He shared with them about His will that was unfolding. Both then talked, believed, and obeyed together. There were no questions or divisive discussion—only obedience *together*. Unity in husband and wife, father and mother, is vital to a healthy family and for healthy and godly children. It also seems obvious that this family was a good steward of their children, as God continued to entrust other sons and daughters (besides Jesus) into their care (Mark 6:3).

God purposed marriage from the very beginning. Joseph and Mary and their children were no exception. They lived as God intended, and God used each and all of them to touch a world forever.

A Marvelous Journey of Faith
by Karen O'Dell Bullock

One of the most significant moments I have experienced with God came during the summer of my thirtieth year. I was a young mother at the time, with two little ones, aged six and three years old. My husband and I had moved to Amarillo, Texas, to be close to my parents and to allow John to finish his last two years of college nearby.

As he completed his undergraduate degree, I taught public school. We were deeply involved in our church and happily settling in to the lovely pattern of life close to parents. During the summer following John's graduation, however, the Father began whispering to my heart, reminding me of His call upon my life—something I had carried deeply within my soul, and known without doubt, since I was a teenager.

I had become aware that God was setting apart my life for some special vocational service during a Vacation Bible School chapel when I was about fifteen. Not knowing exactly what it was, I only sensed that it would involve seminary training and missions. My wonderful, godly pastor-father and mother had affirmed and prayed and encouraged me to follow God's leadership through missions in high school and college.

My husband and I met while we were both summer missionaries, and we married the following year, knowing together that God was calling us into vocational ministry. We then spent more than five years as dorm parents in a ministry that cared for young men who could no longer live at home, and we loved the rural, quiet pace of life on the ranch with these special ones.

During that time our son was born, and three years later, our daughter. I had walked some dark roads, clinging to God, who had proven Himself to be the One who was able to sustain me, to grant peace, and to enable me to overcome some very difficult circumstances. I had grown in my faith and wanted to serve God with everything I knew myself to be.

So here I was, now thirty years old in Amarillo, Texas. God brought me face-to-face with Himself, reminding me of that earlier call. I knew that God was waiting for me to be obedient to take the next step to pursue my seminary education. I also knew that I had been out of school for ten years and that our young children needed their mom to be with them full-time. My heavy responsibilities at church, accompanying the worship teams on the keyboard and evangelism training, were fulfilling but also time-consuming. I was also serving as the accompanist for the Sunday Chapel services where my father preached each week at a nearby hospital. These were good things.

As I prayed alone about these matters, God spoke to my heart and questioned what I was doing in response to the call He had placed on my life. I, myself, would give an answer to that question before His throne some day. I could not stand in another's shoes, or be sanctioned by another's name, or be covered by another's shadow. I would stand alone to answer the God who had put me on this planet, in this time and place in history, to serve Him. That call I had received at fifteen now would be realized both from and within the circles of marriage and family. I spoke with my husband, not knowing at the time that God was speaking to him at the same time about the same thing.

Following a series of amazing events, our little family packed up and came to seminary the following year. I earned the M.Div. and Ph.D. degrees and was then asked to teach. This was what God had in mind for me since the beginning. Today, I still sense God's pleasure most when I grab that silver doorknob to enter the classroom to teach Church History! I am so grateful to Him for allowing me to do for a living what I enjoy most in the world—flipping through the "Father's Family Photo Album" and teaching His people about their heritage.

Two decades ago our young family determined together to be obedient and to follow God, step by step. Was it hard to make that decision without knowing what was going to happen in later years? Oh, yes. Was it costly? Indeed it was . . . in almost every way humanly imaginable. Was it worth the cost? Oh, absolutely! Did we ever look back? Not once. We never regretted the decision in any way. God simply confirmed each day that He knew best and provided for our every need.

Together through these years our family has found that when we followed God in obedience, we came to know Him better. We learned to trust Him more. When we trust God more deeply, our walk with Him grows increasingly sweeter, day by day. It has been a most marvelous journey of faith.

Karen has been a very special person in our lives. When she was a teenager, she came on a mission trip to Saskatoon. She remained connected to our family through the years, attending seminary with our son Richard

*at Southwestern Baptist Theological Seminary and was a mentor for
Carrie, who studied under Karen's teaching and worked for a time as her
grader. Her love for the Lord and for Church history has been an
inspiration to all who have attended her classes. Karen has taught at
Southwestern for fifteen years and is currently the Academic Director of
the Ph.D. in Leadership Studies program at Dallas Baptist University.*

AN EQUALLY YOKED MARRIAGE

God gave a wonderful gift to my life when He brought my wife, Marilynn,
to me. She has been a helpmate in the fullest measure. We have served
together now for more than forty-five years. She "makes up" what I lack
and supports what God has called us to do. She is a people person and very
practical, always helping in a most timely way. She is a great mother to
our five children, and much that they have become is due to her godly and
practical influence and counsel. And now she is significantly affecting the
next generation—our fourteen grandchildren.

There was no way for me to know all that God had in store for my
life when I fell in love with my wife. It was impossible to judge or know
all that God would take us through to further His purposes in our lives.
All I could do was trust that, as God put us together in marriage, He
would keep us together and like-minded as we were obedient to Him.

Today, there is no question in my mind that I would not be where I
am today if it was not for my wife. It would be safe to say that spiritually
I wouldn't be where I am today if I had been unequally yoked in marriage.
My spiritual relationship with the Lord has changed and grown through
the experiences He's brought me through.

What would I have done if my wife had refused to move to the freezing
cold town of Saskatoon? What if she had decided that God wasn't leading
her to leave our comfortable church in Downey, California, where we had

worked so hard? Keeping in mind that we had five children, what if she didn't want to leave our decent salary to go to a church that was putting its building up for sale because of lack of funding? I hear these "reasons" all the time for not following God's will: lack of money or financial security, the church is too small, it is too far away from family, too cold . . . Yet if my wife had been this "reasonable," *Experiencing God* would not have been written the way it was. If I had any doubts about her attitude toward all the time I spent away with church planting, or if I had to worry about the children and having them negatively influenced by my work, I would have been significantly less successful or could have even failed in the ministry.

How important was the verse, "Do not be unequally yoked together"? It was my very life!

Second Corinthians 6:14–16 wasn't meant to limit us, it was meant to free us, to give us freedom to be able to complete God's will without having to choose from being obedient to God and pleasing a spouse. Marriage and the family is so basic to God's purposes from creation that God has revealed specific purposes for the husband, for the wife, and even for the children. For when you are united in marriage, those bonds—for better or worse—will have an effect on your response to God and what He will do in your life.

Joseph had to work through many obstacles as a husband. Being a respected and godly man, Joseph had the right to expect to marry a "pure" woman. Although the angel went to him revealing God's plan and purpose for Mary, there is no mention that the angel went to the rest of the town to explain! Joseph's betrothed was clearly with child in this strict and law-abiding society. This could have affected his relationship with his family and even his work, which was dependent on having customers. If Joseph's family was still dealing with the shame of this marriage, it might also explain why there was no family present at the birth of Jesus.

Because of his love for God and possibly his love for Mary, he thought nothing of others' opinions but was obedient to God's revealed will for his life. His walk with God, especially in his knowledge and obedience to the truth in Scripture, would dramatically affect the family as a whole and each one individually. He was to be the protector and provider of the home. Even with the little we know of his life from Scripture, it is obvious he met these God-purposed responsibilities. He also was to be the primary teacher in the home, and Jesus' knowledge of Scripture indicated that Joseph faithfully taught his children as God commanded (Deut. 6; Ps. 78).

Our example of Joseph and Mary's marriage is so important in seeing how God puts people together to form a family. Their way was not easy! They had so many hindrances that could have led to disobedience—but they didn't. Just as Joseph had to trust Mary, Mary also had to trust Joseph. She allowed him to be the spiritual leader, and she was also a part of the obedience as God led Joseph. It is interesting that after Joseph took responsibility of Mary, it was Joseph who then received the instructions for his family from the Lord. God could have continued to show Himself to Mary but chose to follow His pattern for marriage.

God knew that Mary needed a godly husband because the husband often determines the spiritual maturity and health of his wife and family. If you are in some form of church work, it is doubly important that you and your spouse be unified and growing together.

Today, family life is falling apart dramatically, even in the homes of God's people. This is grievous to God. He is glorified when our lives demonstrate Him fully—His nature, ways, purposes, and activity. He is profaned before a watching world when we do not demonstrate the difference He makes in our lives (see Ezek. 36:23–27). When the father and mother live godly lives, as Joseph and Mary did, the family and the family witness is strong. It will even encourage other shaky families to be strengthened.

Scripture, not merely the prevailing culture, must once again shape our lives. And husbands and wives must be better models of what God intended the marriage to be—especially to their own children. When God has a couple or family that is seeking after Him with an obedient heart, He has a family that He will work through to make a difference in His kingdom!

QUESTIONS FOR STUDY AND RESPONSE

1. The family was always in God's eternal plan. It is no surprise that He placed Mary with Joseph, committing to them the task of giving Jesus a solid foundation from which to grow. Has God given you a life partner? If so, thank Him and seek to be the person God needs you to be in order for the other to be free to follow God. If not, thank the Lord that He has chosen to meet your needs Himself!

2. When God encountered Mary, her ability to complete God's plan for her life rested on her husband's obedience. Joseph had to obey the Lord as well, giving the support, guidance, and direction Mary needed—especially after the birth of Jesus. When God reveals His plans to us, we also need support and guidance from our spouse. If you are married, have you been that support, always encouraging the other to seek after God in obedience? Have you made sure that your spouse has been true to the Lord in what He has revealed? As a life partner, it is our responsibility to support and encourage each other and help each other to fulfill our vows to the Lord.

3. Mary and Joseph had to stand together to be fully obedient to the Lord. What God had told Mary was enough for Joseph, and what God had revealed to Joseph was enough for Mary to also obey. Mary didn't need a special revelation to know that Herod was seeking to kill her son; God had already told Joseph! Have you taken seriously what God has revealed to your spouse? Do you see God's revelation to your spouse as a revelation to you as well?

4. The religious culture of Joseph and Mary's day gave strong directives in a walk with God from an early age. How would you rate the effectiveness of the religious culture in our day in its influence on our walk with God?

5. Scripture greatly influenced the lives of Joseph, Mary, and Jesus. Sadly, among many of God's people today there seems to be a void of scriptural knowledge and understanding. How did this come about? How strong and deep is your scriptural knowledge? How are the Scriptures affecting your marriage in practical ways?

6. In order for society to be stable and resilient, family life must be strong. On a scale of 1–10, rate the following:

_____ your marriage in light of Mary and Joseph's example

_____ your family and its influence on others

_____ your role, or your responsibility, in helping your spouse grow spiritually

_____ your obedience to the Lord in your marriage

CHAPTER 4

IN GOD'S FULLNESS
OF TIME

But when the fullness of the time had come, God sent forth His Son,
born of a woman, born under the law, to redeem those who were
under the law, that we might receive the adoption as sons.
—GALATIONS 4:4–5

SALVATION WAS COMING to God's people. What a wonderful and exciting time to be living in! The promise given from the Father was being fulfilled, and the world would see God's love and mercy lived out in front of their very eyes. It had always been God's plan that He would send His Son into the world and that He would redeem those who believed in Him. He even gave many prophecies in the Old Testament Scripture so that the nature and the way in which Jesus came would be clear. In fact, God gave the way Christ would come, His genealogy so people would recognize His lineage, where He would be born and where He would live, the approach of His life and ministry, and even the manner of His death! God had every plan in place and brought together every detail for this very time. God's fullness of this time would only come once in history, so it is important to understand all of God's preparation for His Son and for Mary, who lived her life in God's "fullness of time."

THE ROMAN EMPIRE

During this time in history, the Roman Empire was entering an incredible era of change. Because of the Greek influence of previous centuries, this Greco-Roman culture used Greek as the language of business and Roman for ordinary communication.[1] So in this fullness of time, the Gospel could be preached to all peoples in the entire world through this common language.

Under the Romans, major roadways were constructed, crisscrossing through Palestine and on to many key cities throughout the known world. The roads were safe and available for God's good news to be taken to every nation. Major cities were being built until the entire Mediterranean world was urbanized.

The Romans, through this time period, were able to unite this world under one political structure and one common language, allowing for a free-moving society.[2] All of these factors left the world ripe for the hearing and spreading of the gospel of Christ. Also, this political structure and its census for taxation is what required Joseph and his family to endure the trip to Bethlehem. Thus, God used the Roman government to help fulfill His purposes, and they became "an instrument for fulfilling His prophecies."[3] It was God's fullness of time!

THE PROPHECIES CONCERNING CHRIST

Many different Old Testament Scriptures were given to help prepare the people for the manner in which Christ would come. Genesis 12:3 and Genesis 17:19 mention that through Abraham and Isaac's lineage, all the earth shall be blessed. Numbers 24:17 had a more specific indication of the Messiah: "I see Him, but not now; I behold Him, but not near; a Star shall come out of Jacob; a Scepter shall rise out of Israel . . ."

54

Genesis 49:10 also mentions this same Scepter out of Judah: "The scepter shall not depart from Judah, nor a lawgiver from between his feet, until Shiloh comes; and to Him shall be the obedience of the people."

Isaiah gives us several passages in which the Savior's coming is described with specific details. Beginning in Isaiah 9:6–7, we are told,

> For unto us a Child is born, unto us a Son is given; and the government will be upon His shoulder. And His name will be called Wonderful, Counselor, Mighty God, Everlasting Father, Prince of Peace. Of the increase of His government and peace there will be no end, upon the throne of David and over his kingdom, to order it and establish it with judgment and justice from that time forward, even forever. The zeal of the Lord of hosts will perform this.

Isaiah 7:14 gives us a specific sign for Christ's birth. It says, "The Lord Himself will give you a sign: Behold, the virgin shall conceive and bear a Son, and shall call His name Immanuel . . ."

Micah 5:2 tells us, "Bethlehem . . . though you are little among the thousands of Judah, yet out of you shall come forth to Me the One to be Ruler in Israel, whose goings forth are from of old, from everlasting."

Hosea 11:1 mentions that the Son will be called out of Egypt, and in a powerful passage in Jeremiah, even the slaughter of the children that would follow Jesus' birth is foretold (31:15).

The wonderful mystery of the Scripture is that it must be understood through faith. How is it that so many people can read the Scriptures, and some are granted understanding of God's revelation while others miss it completely? Mary (highly favored one), Joseph (a just man), Simeon (who was just and devout), Anna the prophetess (who did not depart from the temple but served God with fastings and prayers night and day), Elizabeth and Zacharias (who were righteous and blameless)—these were people who understood the laws and prophets and adjusted their lives to what God was doing. It seems clear that in order for the Father to teach us from the Scriptures, we must have a heart that is willing to learn, listen, and obey. And God will instruct and guide us in "His fullness of time" throughout our lifetime.

This same principle will continue to be constant in the days to come. Whenever we see God working around us, every detail is in place and the time is complete. This will also certainly be true concerning Christ's final coming.

THE RELIGIOUS CLIMATE

There was an amazing factor in the religious climate of the days of Joseph and Mary. God's people had been taken into captivity because of their sin against God, and they were persecuted and in bondage for centuries. During this time strong religious sects arose, including the Pharisees. They were zealous for God and purity towards the Law. Then the scribes and Levites taught the people the Law and led them to have a strong longing for and a heart cry for the Messiah to come. He would come as a triumphant King on David's throne and defeat their enemies, setting up His kingdom and reigning with power once again. He would once again bring peace and prosperity. This was one of the strongest longings and hopes in God's people at this time. However, their expectations were mostly for political freedom and not spiritual restoration.

Everything in Scripture pointed to a Messiah's reign, and the religious leaders had used the Scripture to shape it after their own traditions and reasoning. Because of this, they missed God's Messiah, His own Son, Jesus. The tragedy and sorrow that would pass over Mary's soul would come because of the religious leaders' expectations that were not of Scripture, but of tradition. Later Jesus would warn them of this:

Whenever you see a cloud rising out of the west, immediately you say, "A shower is coming"; and so it is. And when you see the south wind blow, you say, "There will be hot weather"; and there is. Hypocrites! You can discern the face of the sky and of the earth, but how is it you do not discern this time? (Luke 12:54–56)

So blind were the religious leaders to God's presence that they killed Jesus and brought about the destruction of Jerusalem—because they did not recognize the time of God's coming (Luke 19:44).

This was the intense spiritual time in which Joseph and Mary brought Jesus into the world. This is the mystery of God's fullness of time.

Historically, God's timing for revival is often in the "worst of times" spiritually. How important it is for God's people to be keenly and faithfully walking with God in His fullness of time!

ZACHARIAS AND ELIZABETH

Although we have already discussed Zacharias and Elizabeth at length, we must again understand and realize how God worked in their lives in His perfect timing. There were so many considerations and details that God was bringing together in a manner that only He could do. All this activity of God would require faith in everyone who would know God's salvation (Heb. 2:1–2).

God gave both Zacharias and Elizabeth a godly heritage from a priestly line. He united them in marriage and united their hearts to serve Him. God withheld both the blessing of having a child and that of serving the people as the temple priest until His timing was complete. He walked them through their circumstances, teaching and preparing them to be among the greatest influences on Mary's young life. All of these steps were essential in God's eternal plan! Only God and the ones involved knew this activity of

God's to bring His salvation to the world. (It is so exciting to see is how God unfolded His plan of salvation—in His timing.)

God, who at various times and in various ways spoke in time past to the fathers by the prophets, has in these last days spoken to us by His Son, whom He has appointed heir of all things, through whom also He made the worlds . . . when He had by Himself purged our sins, sat down at the right hand of the Majesty on high, having become so much better than the angels, as He has by inheritance obtained a more excellent name than they. (Heb. 1:1–2, 3–4)

When Mary was of age to be betrothed, God set in motion His redemption. Elizabeth's child was to prepare the way of the Lord. In a touching passage of Scripture, we hear the importance of the announcement to Zacharias concerning his son, John the Baptist:

Do not be afraid, Zacharias, for your prayer is heard; and your wife Elizabeth will bear you a son, and you shall call his name John. And you will have joy and gladness, and many will rejoice at his birth. For he will be great in the sight of the Lord, and shall drink neither wine nor strong drink. He will also be filled with the Holy Spirit, even from his mother's womb. And he will turn many of the children of Israel to the Lord their God. He will also go before Him in the spirit and power of Elijah, "to turn the hearts of the fathers to the children," and the disobedient to the wisdom of the just, to make ready a people prepared for the Lord. (Luke 1:13–17)

Zacharias and Elizabeth were experiencing in their lives God's perfect timing in His purpose to redeem a lost world.

When Christ's birth was announced to Mary, God's messenger used Elizabeth's pregnancy as a sign to her that what she was hearing was true. Mary quickly went to Elizabeth and Zacharias's house and found the truth. God had prepared these two to be a blessing to Mary and help encourage and instruct her in her faith. She stayed under their instruction for three months. What a difference this would make in Mary's young life. God brought all these details together—in His fullness of time!

JOSEPH AND MARY

Scripture gives us enough information to understand some important facts about Joseph, as we discussed in chapter 3. God had prepared his priestly heritage to also come from the line of David (Matt. 1:1–17). He would have come from a family that respected the Scriptures and the Law and one that had clearly instructed him in the ways of God. We are told that Joseph was a "just man" (v. 19). He was the one God trusted to instruct His Son in the ways of God. Three encounters are recorded in Scripture where God's messenger came, instructed Joseph in what God would have him do, and Joseph responded immediately in obedience. Without his yielded heart to God and His activity, Joseph could have had Mary stoned to death for disgracing him and his family! Instead, he didn't question what he was told but followed in obedience, possibly enduring ridicule and shame along with Mary. When everything seems so out of place, it can often be God working around you. This is where most people miss God and His activity in their lives.

God had visibly been preparing Mary's heart for this incredible time in history. God placed her in a God-honoring family that trained her in the ways of the Scripture. Mary was very faithful to all of God's laws. Several times the Gospels mention that "they had performed all things according to the law of the Lord" (Luke 2:39).

When the angel brought God's words to Mary, God had already marshaled all of heaven and had prepared every detail for the coming of His Son! He had already been at work in the lives of Elizabeth and Zacharias, having encountered them six months earlier when the angel foretold the coming of their son, John—who was to prepare the way for the coming Messiah. John's life also had been foretold in Scripture (Isa. 40:3). They were ready to encourage and instruct Mary. When God encountered Mary, that was the time for her to act!

"Come now, and let us reason together," says the LORD, "Though your sins are like scarlet, they shall be as white as snow; though they are red like crimson, they shall be as wool. If you are willing and obedient, you shall eat the good of the land; but if you refuse and rebel, you shall be devoured by the sword"; for the mouth of the LORD has spoken. (Isa. 1:18–20)

God had unmistakably prepared both Joseph and Mary for this moment in history, and they had prepared their hearts to follow their God in obedience.

Encountering God Through My Daily Walk
by Pamel T. Kirkland

For my fiftieth birthday, I chose my outfit carefully—red and purple associated with the coming of the age. I had my roots done—because no one going over the hill wants gray showing. At the party several had been asked to speak. One comment from the minister I had worked with for twenty-nine years caught me off guard, "She thinks like a man, works like a horse, and acts like a lady."

Late that night in my "pondering mode" I found the three statements to be particularly intriguing, yet flattering. I thought about where I had been and where I could have gone. I thanked God for the different people in my life that He used to guide me toward Him. And I praised Him that I continually have the opportunity to observe His church at work on a firsthand basis.

My pastor taught us that when we pray, we should list our petitions on one side and praises on the other side. This has helped make my prayer time more effective and proved beneficial in this evaluation with the Lord on my fifty years of life. For example, the year alcohol claimed the life of my mother, I had accepted Christ just four months earlier at the invitation of my best friend to attend Vacation Bible School. The year I had a hysterectomy, our daughter accepted Christ. The same year my daddy died, our first grandchild was born. I had heard life is either going into a storm, is already in a storm, or is preparing for a storm. That is why it is so important to acknowledge the presence of God in your life every day. Through the years God has always used my fears and weaknesses to draw me nearer to Him.

- He used my fearful spirit to make me afraid of alcohol. Others in my family have found it as a wrong refuge.
- He used my fear of divorce to strengthen my marriage.
- He took my hurt over not being able to have other children and gave me friends that shared theirs. Our home is like a second home to many.
- Even though I became a Christian as a teenager and did not have a wealth of Bible knowledge, He gave me a ministry opportunity as a pastor's assistant.

- He used my recognition of my insecurities to help raise an independent daughter.
- He used my fear of death by allowing me to be at the bedside of my aunt, at the foot of Daddy's hospital bed, and by the side of my father-in-law as they left this world to enter heaven's glory.

As a pastor's assistant, when I feel caught in the hectic days with the pendulum of emotions that come with each phone call, I am reminded of Galatians 6:9–10: "Let us not grow weary while doing good, for in due season we shall reap if we do not lose heart. Therefore, as we have opportunity, let us do good to all, especially to those who are of the household of faith."

I don't want to be like the last dab of peanut butter left in the jar, the unused software, or the banana that sits and rots. It would be awful to reach heaven and have the Lord tell me, "I gave you all these talents, and you wasted several." I want to be like the woman who poured the expensive oil on the Master: Let me be "broken and spilled out . . . and used up for Thee."

In that late-night discussion with the Lord in reflection of the past, inspection of the present, and affirmation of the future, I remembered again how God drew me closer to Him through a sermon on the responsibility of influence. The pastor made it very clear that even to sit in a corner and never speak was an influence. That radically changed my thinking and my accountability for my Christian walk. Whether I am consoling a dear soul in the loss of a loved one, calming down a nervous bride and/or her mother, or helping a new convert into the baptismal waters, it is my desire to always let others see Jesus in me.

I am so thankful for all the people who remained faithful to the Lord and helped me come to a deeper understanding of who God is.

God used a combination of seemingly small events to bring me to Him: Sunday school, church mission programs, a caring church staff member, special events at church . . . All of these were what God used as stepping stones to where I am today.

I praise God that I am a woman—emotional, methodical, and unpredictable—but it is so awesome that He made women that way. As mothers we can understand creation uniquely as we experience the birth of our children. God wired us for high awareness of needs and equipped us with vast capabilities. We can be meek and submissive to the wonderful men in our lives, yet stand beside them and support them to be all God wants them to be.

And as far as, "Think like a man, work like a horse, and act like a lady"—anything less would be an embarrassment as I strive to encounter God daily and stay in the center of His will for my life.

Pam has truly been a blessing and a trusted friend. She will probably never know how much she has quietly influenced all those around her, but we know that her love for the Lord has impacted many. We deeply appreciate her example as one who lives her life in Christ to the fullest!

AN URGENCY TO OBEY

God without a doubt brought Marilynn and me (Henry) together. We were both very fortunate to have godly parents who lived out God's claim and call on their lives. And because of this, we both had the same sense of divine mission in our lives. This has shaped our lives together, as God did with Joseph and Mary.

This has been worked out in many ways in my life. Throughout my life I have always sensed an urgency to obey the Lord immediately. His calling me to work with CEOs and His call for me to be involved with the United Nations and the military have all come when God Himself is about to move in mighty ways. I have an increasing sense that if I do not quickly adjust my life when God reveals to me His will, then I will not be ready or prepared to impact eternity with those who are facing a crisis in their lives.

God's call for me to write and then equipping my children to write with me is always God-initiated. Each book I have written I have sensed, "Now this book is in God's special fullness of time!" In other words, when the opportunities to write a book arise, God has a special plan and purpose for each one's writing. Then as the books are being written, I am watching specific lives being changed, called, and affected right on schedule to them—and, of course, to God.

Throughout Scripture, whether in the creation accounts in Genesis or through to the final return of our Lord in Revelation, God moves and acts in His "fullness of time." Mary was chosen to be in the midst of God's fullness of time and experienced the work of the Lord through her life: "But when the fullness of the time had come, God sent forth His Son, born of a woman, born under the law, to redeem those who were under the law, that we might receive the adoption as sons" (Gal. 4:4–5).

God always acts in history and always in His fullness of time—that is, in His timing. This is absolutely true for us as well. No activity of God in our lives is haphazard or accidental. Instead, it is always purposeful and timely. Therefore it is crucial that we respond immediately and thoroughly—and with joy and awe.

**No activity of God in our lives is haphazard or
accidental. Instead, it is always purposeful and timely.
Therefore it is crucial that we respond immediately and
thoroughly—and with joy and awe.**

When we consider God's fullness of time, we think not only of Mary but of all God's people affected in history. Another example of God's timing is seen in the moment God announced to Moses His fullness of time for His oppressed people:

> I have surely seen the oppression of My people who are in Egypt, and have heard their cry because of their taskmasters, for I know their sorrows. So I have come down to deliver them out of the hand of the Egyptians, and to bring them up from that land to a good and large land, to a land flowing with milk and honey. (Exod. 3:7–8)

God sent Moses as His instrument to deliver His people. Moses experienced God's fullness of time as God used his life to deliver God's people from the oppression of the Egyptians.

When God sent His prophets, it was always in God's crucial fullness of time. When the Israelites were oppressed or captive or experiencing great difficulty, they cried out to the Lord, who would send them a deliverer in the form of a prophet. This was a continuing cycle for many years.

When Jesus called and trained twelve apostles, God was preparing them to be the leaders of His people. It was crucial that they had the time and grounding with Christ and His teachings. It was after they were prepared by God that the Holy Spirit came and the first churches were begun. God's timing in the calling of the apostle Paul was no accident or surprise! It was all in God's fullness of time.

When God encounters us individually, He has already set the stage for His activity. And when He speaks, that is His fullness of time! He has brought everything together in history, in our circumstances, in our physical and spiritual lives. He has left nothing out, and He has thought through and prepared every detail. When He speaks to us, that moment is the very time to respond in complete obedience to His words. Make no mistake—this moment in history, or even in this time of your life, will never come again. It will not come again in the life of your children. Don't miss the fullness of all that God intends for your life and the life of your family because you didn't prepare your heart for obedience.

QUESTIONS FOR STUDY AND RESPONSE

1. As Mary's life unfolded, she saw God's activity to its completion and marveled. We can also see God working in our lives and in those around us every day. Have you taken time to marvel in God's presence? Do you also share the awe of having God work in and through your life? Take time in God's presence and remember the wonder of the God of the universe choosing to work through your life!

2. When God encounters our lives, He has thought through every detail and comes to us exactly when we need to understand His ways. Do you see God's involvement with you as His fullness of time and understand the importance for you to respond immediately with obedience?

3. When God came to Mary, it was with a specific purpose to reveal His plan to use her life for His glory. This plan would ultimately affect the course of history! When we experience God working in our lives, it is with a specific purpose. Do you have a sense of excitement watching to see what God is doing, and therefore how special His fullness of time is with you? Have you seen God working out the details of your life for a purpose? Look to see God, not just in the big or important moments, but also in the daily, quiet details of your life.

4. Mary did not struggle or wrestle with God's plan for her life. God did not have to wait for an answer while Mary contemplated the pros and cons of agreeing to God's will. She believed what He said

was true and then set about to obey. Can you remember a time in your life when God came to you, yet you wasted valuable time in responding obediently? Have you struggled over a decision that God has given you, only to find that it was too late and had already passed you by? If so, ask the Lord to forgive you, and commit your heart to always respond to the Lord with an immediate yes.

CHAPTER 5

TO BE CHOSEN BY GOD IS TO BE HIGHLY FAVORED

*But when it pleased God, who separated me from my mother's
womb and called me through His grace, to reveal His Son in me,
that I might preach Him among the Gentiles . . .*
—GALATIONS 1:15–16

I (CARRIE) CAN POINT to many occasions when God unexpectedly
showed me favor. When I was fifteen, my wonderfully planned summer
vacation was interrupted for a trip to Glorieta, New Mexico. My father
was scheduled to speak at the Foreign Missions Week (now known as
International Missions Week) at the Southern Baptist Convention's
conference center and, because I was too young to stay by myself at fifteen, I attended the meetings as well. I have always enjoyed hearing my
father speak, so when the evening service came I was listening and hop-
ing to learn more about the Lord. Was I ever surprised when I not only
learned about the Lord, but I encountered Him in a real and personal
way. It was during one of the commitment services that I felt God grip
my heart and call me into His service for missions. He touched me so
powerfully that I never forgot that moment.

In fact, God has used this time to keep me steadily on His path for my life. This encounter with my Lord encouraged me six months later when I found out I had cancer. When I faced difficulties in university, I remembered the time when God clearly called me to follow Him in ministry and mission work. Now, it is no surprise to me that I am serving with the International Mission Board almost twenty years after the initial call. God chose to reveal Himself to me in a timely way in my life, and He has encouraged me through the years to remain fixed on Him. He continues to bless my life, though I don't deserve it. This is what it means to be a child of God! He wants to choose us, bless us, and give us His fullness of life.

MARY'S MESSAGE FROM HEAVEN

For Mary, God Himself had sent a message from His heart, revealing what He was about to do in her life. He had an immediate purpose to fulfill. Gabriel, the same angel who spoke to Zacharias and previously to Daniel (Dan. 9:20–23), had come to Mary with good news for her. Out of all the people on the earth at this time, God chose to come to Mary. She had "found favor with God." What an incredible moment for her! God had set His love upon her, and she now would be the focus of the activity of God in her and through her. Perfect love would now rest upon her, and the angel reassured her.

> Then the angel said to her, "Do not be afraid, Mary, for you have found favor with God. And behold, you will conceive in your womb and bring forth a Son, and shall call His name Jesus. He will be great, and will be called the Son of the Highest; and the Lord God will give Him the throne of His father David." (Luke 1:30–33)

The angel further assured her that "the Holy Spirit will come upon you, and the power of the Highest will overshadow you" (Luke 1:35).

Therefore, to "find favor with God" meant that God Himself would be actively at work in her, and then through her, accomplishing His eternal purposes. His purpose for Mary was to entrust His Son to her, helping and equipping her to raise Jesus to be obedient to the Father—even unto death. The "favor" didn't end with just the revelation, but continued throughout her life, guiding and helping her to fulfill the task for which she was chosen. When God chooses a life through whom He will work, it is clear, thorough, timely, and always accompanied by His enabling grace. The choice by God is always an expression of His favor. His favor also means "the Lord is with you" (Luke 1:28).

"I am Gabriel, who stands in the presence of God, and was sent to speak to you and bring you these glad tidings." (Luke 1:19)

Heaven has known the eternal significance of this. What God announces, He Himself does. "The LORD of hosts has sworn, saying, 'Surely, as I have thought, so it shall come to pass, and as I have purposed, so it shall stand'" (Isa. 14:24). He spoke in creation, and He brought it about. He is always present to bring His expressed will to pass when He speaks. With Mary, Gabriel assured her that "the Holy Spirit will come upon you, and the power of the Highest will overshadow you" (Luke 1:35).

God did not merely assure her that an angel would be with her. The angel assured her God Himself would be with her. Everyone God chooses can be assured of God Himself being with them to enable them in all things, at all times.

When God calls us, His work doesn't end with the call. That is just the beginning. When He shows His favor, you can be sure that He will continue to prepare, direct, equip, and sustain you to complete the task He's given—and He will complete it *through* you! This is true in the life of every child of God whom He calls for His purposes.

It is important to understand that when we refer to "the call," we are not only talking about a call into full-time Christian service. God places His people in every walk of life. Whether you are in teaching, business, health care, or a homemaker, God can use you. Mary remained a homemaker, and God used her there in mighty ways. Raising a child God will use in our world for His purposes is most significant.

> **God places His people in every walk of life. Whether you are in teaching, business, health care, or a homemaker, God can use you . . . Raising a child God will use in our world for His purposes is most significant.**

God can call you regardless of your education, status, heritage, job, or even lack of a job. God is working to save people in the marketplace, in the universities, and in every neighborhood, town, and village. Age, whether young or old, is not a deciding factor on whether God can use you—God is looking at your heart. There are no "unimportant" people in God's creation. Regardless of where you are in life, God calls His people to His purposes.

Every child of God should be seeking to obey the Lord and all that He has for life. When you are obedient in the little things, He will entrust you with more. And when your obedience is proven through the bigger things, your assignment will continue to grow to match your obedience.

A Moment That Changed My Life
by Minuette Drumwright Pratt

I grew up surrounded by prayer in my home and my church, where my dad was pastor of the same little church in San Antonio for twenty-five years. It was a typical Baptist church for that era—small, evangelistic, missions minded, at least two revivals a year. At our home, we had many rules—including no card playing (except Old Maid), no dancing, no movies, and no exceptions. My parents believed in punishment when rules were broken—with a peach tree switch. I even got a switching one day when I said, "Oh, look, our *switch* tree has a *peach* on it!" One of those many rules had to do with being a smart aleck. That was the rule that got me in the most trouble!

However, my home and my church gave me many opportunities to learn the things of the Lord. I memorized quite a few Bible verses. I did pretty well in sword drill and fulfilled all the steps in Girls Auxiliary. (My Queen Regent cape is still hanging in my closet!) At the age of nine, I sincerely asked Jesus to forgive my sins and come live in my heart. To borrow someone else's words, "All that I understood of myself, I gave to all that I understood of Jesus." It was not much I understood, but I meant it.

Now, I believed in prayer. And I prayed. However, I know now, in retrospect, that deep down, in the years that followed, there was not much going on *in my soul*. I went off to college (no peach trees there!), and the exciting day eventually came when I married a seminary student, Huber Drumwright. Soon, he was teaching New Testament and Greek at Southwestern Seminary. After six years, Huber was eligible for a sabbatical leave. He chose to go to Princeton Seminary in order to pursue postdoctoral work—which eventually produced a Greek grammar.

When we arrived, I took advantage of a last-minute opportunity to take a class on "Prayer and Worship." I was not really expecting to encounter anything new. After all, I had grown up in the middle of prayer. Yet the Lord used that godly professor and his gentle, probing questions to lead me into a time of *major* self-inventory. In that process, I made some disturbing discoveries about myself. I discovered I was *shallow* in my understanding of the real meaning and purpose of prayer. Therefore, I was *shallow* in my relationship with the God of prayer. Further, I was *inconsistent* in spending quality time with Him in prayer. Therefore, I was *lacking* in the spiritual energy and divine direction that authentic devotion and closeness to God bring into one's everyday living.

Shallow, inconsistent, lacking. That was hard to take. Here I was a pastor's daughter, the wife of a seminary professor. And, actually, at that very time, I was teaching a book on prayer to a local group of women! I felt brokenness before the Lord as I caught a glimpse of myself as God saw me—I was "a mile wide and an inch deep." It was then that I discerned the words of Jesus saying lovingly, "Learn of Me." I knew I wanted to. With all my heart, I wanted to. I asked Him to become my daily Teacher. He is still teaching me. And, even now that I am older, I'm still learning from Him.

Now I give myself a periodic reality check. Is there shallowness and inconsistency in my soul? Is prayer only a ritual, a nice grouping of routine, prayer-type words, a casual matter? Am I praying only with my lips, or is it my life that prays? Is a growing intimacy with God in Christ taking place deep within? Am I only going through the motions of prayer? Have I become pretty good at looking better on the outside than I really am on the inside? Richard Foster wrote, "The great need today is not for more intelligent people or more gifted people. The great need today is for deeper people." Are you among the deep people? And again I ask myself: *Am I?*

Note: Dr. Drumwright, Minette's husband for thirty years, died in 1981. In 2003, Minette fell in love again and married Dr. William Pratt.

Minette served for many years as the prayer strategist for the Foreign Mission Board of the Southern Baptist Convention (now IMB) and worked alongside T. W. Hunt, my (Carrie's) father, and others. As a young teen, I saw the three of them pray together, seeking God's heart for revival and spiritual awakening, and it had a powerful impact on my life. Minette's gracious spirit and love for the Lord made a deep and lasting impression in my heart, which continues to this day. She is the author of When My Faith Feels Shallow: Pursuing the Depths of God *and* The Life that Prays: Reflections on Prayer as Strategy.

God is always at work around us, seeking to bring people to Himself. Because He chooses to do this through His own people, we as Christians should have many times in our lives where we can look back and say, "God so richly used and blessed my life when . . ."

HANNAH'S PRAYER

A good example in the Old Testament of God showing His favor is in the life of little Samuel. God told him, "I will raise up for Myself a faithful priest who shall do according to what is in My heart and in My mind. I will build him a sure house, and he shall walk before My anointed forever" (1 Sam. 2:35).

Samuel's life was a direct answer to his mother Hannah's prayer, and he was dedicated and raised to be God's servant. God saw Hannah's heart and entrusted her to raise a great prophet at a crucial time in Israel's history. When Samuel was still very young, God chose to speak to him and reveal His purposes for His people, seeking to draw them back into a pure relationship with Him. Samuel then chose to faithfully share God's will. As he accurately relayed all that God told him, God continued to use Samuel as a prophet to turn God's people back to the Lord.

As Samuel grew, his obedience continued, and so did God's favor and trust that he would be faithful in bigger assignments. And all the people knew that Samuel walked with God because he allowed the Lord to work through him.[1] "So Samuel grew, and the LORD was with him and let none of his words fall to the ground. And all Israel from Dan to Beersheba knew that Samuel had been established as a prophet of the LORD" (1 Sam. 3:19–20).

This pattern with Samuel can be seen throughout the Scripture. It is clear and simple: God has something in mind that He wishes to happen. He chooses someone through whom He will do this. He calls that person and announces or shares with him or her His purposes. That person has been singled out for such an enormous blessing to experience God in a special and unique manner. This individual must now decide whether what he has experienced is from God. When God's people obey, God accomplishes His purposes through them. What a completely overwhelming experience, but one that is not difficult to see or understand. It is also significant that God chooses a godly woman, like Hannah and Mary, to be the mother who will faithfully raise a child God plans to use.

He also chose David His servant, and took him from the sheepfolds; from following the ewes that had young He brought him, to shepherd Jacob His people, and Israel His inheritance. (Ps. 78:70–71)

THE INVOLVEMENT OF OTHERS

At this time in my life, I (Henry) carry a huge sense that God has indeed chosen to show His favor on me and my life and family. I have sensed this for years but have not known how to fully appreciate it. I have noticed some things that accompany such a call of God. First, God places companions and many friends in my life. A life chosen by God involves others. Wherever God places you, others get involved. While in Saskatoon many people—college students, individuals, and churches—felt led of God to come over and help us. This affected our lives permanently and deeply helped each of our children. To this day (like the apostle Paul) we have lasting friendships for every area of our lives.

Further, to be favored by God opened my eyes and heart to the promises of God that accompany the call and that bring great joy in the fulfillment of it. But also, such favor calls for great stewardship. Such stewardship has called forth the writing of many books to bear witness to God's mercy and grace and to encourage God's people in their pilgrimage. I have chosen "not to receive the grace of God in vain" (2 Cor. 6:1 AMP).

Any time that God reveals Himself, His plans, or His way to us, we have been shown favor from God. The favor of God is His alone to grant and remains His sovereign choice. Whatever God asks us to do, whether a lofty or seemingly lowly task, we must remember that the God of the universe has chosen to work through us! He doesn't have to use us at all and could leave us out of His plans, but He wants us to know Him in a deeper and more meaningful way. It is important to always remember what God said to His people about the uniqueness of their relationship with Him:

> You are a holy people to the LORD your God; the LORD your God has chosen you to be a people for Himself, a special treasure above all the peoples on the face of the earth. The LORD did not set His love on you nor choose you because you were more in number than any other people, for you were the least of all peoples; but because the LORD loves you, and because He would keep the oath which He swore to your fathers. (Deut. 7:6–8)

Today, anything that we are called to do is a sovereign choice of God. God can choose to work in and through any of His people who have their hearts set on obeying Him. He will call people in every walk of life, regardless of their job, position or status, wealth, education, or age. Every Christian has the opportunity to be used of God, and He will use those who determine to respond in obedience when He chooses to show His favor on their lives. It is important to understand that without God choosing to reveal Himself to us, we would be nothing of eternal value in God's kingdom (John 15:15). God is so good in allowing us to be involved in His work! And He will always give His best to those who recognize His divine calling in their lives and obey immediately.

God's favor on your life will also affect the lives around you. Never doubt that when God deeply touches your life, not only will others notice, but they will also have to make the decision to be involved in your life and what God is doing—or not! God can use you to bring about a deep blessing to your family, friends, neighbors, coworkers, and especially your church family as He seeks to bring you closer to Himself. God's choice of Mary blessed all those around her as well as others throughout history.

QUESTIONS FOR STUDY AND RESPONSE

1. Any encounter with God is special and shows that you also have been highly favored. Can you recall such a time in your life?

2. When God does show His favor by calling you, He always promises to send His equipping power to help you complete the task. Have you ever allowed your feelings of inadequacy to keep you from obeying God's call on your life?

3. Have you ever felt that God had given you a task, and you followed Him in obedience and saw Him do amazing things through your life? Take time to remember what God has done and thank Him for choosing to use you.

4. Can you remember a time in your life when you felt that God gave you a task, but you did not follow through in obedience? Or have you felt that your Christian walk has been "stilted" or that you haven't grown in your walk with the Lord recently? Take time to examine if you have been disobedient. Ask the Lord to forgive you and set your heart to follow Him in obedience. You can't go back and change the past, but God will help you start again and give you a new beginning with Him.

CHAPTER 6

FEATURES OF AN ENCOUNTER WITH GOD

Do not look at his appearance or at his physical stature, because I have refused him. For the LORD does not see as man sees; for man looks at the outward appearance, but the LORD looks at the heart.

—1 SAMUEL 16:7

I (HENRY) HAD A LIFE-CHANGING ENCOUNTER with God when I was about nine years of age. While I was praying, God suddenly showed me clearly and thoroughly that He was God and I was not! To a young boy, this was clear and simple and life-determining. I have never gotten over the encounter or the radical implications of it all. It affected the way I looked on life—sports, vocation, friends, serving God—and gave me a very serious outlook at all of life. I sensed from that time (though the fuller meaning had to unfold with the passing of time and events) that I was seeing life much differently than many around me. I saw others struggling and wrestling with God over these same decisions that had become obvious choices to me in following God's will. I had but one question: Was this God's will for me? If I knew that the assignment was from the Lord, the answer has always been an immediate "Yes, Lord!"

We as Christians have a desire to serve the Lord and encounter Him in a special way. Many of us want to say as Mary did, "Behold the maid-servant of the Lord! Let it be to me according to your word" (Luke 1:38). Yet it sometimes may seem that God is not answering our prayers or that there is something missing in our lives. It is important to see all the aspects of God's encounter with Mary to give us a broader understanding of how God encounters our lives.

The first thing that we notice is that God's ways are not our ways. Often, we joke that it would be much easier if God would just call us on the phone! It certainly would seem an easier and less complicated way for us to discern His will for our lives. Yet God is God, and His ways are completely different from anything we could think or imagine. Isaiah 55:8–9 says, "'For My thoughts are not your thoughts, nor are your ways My ways,' says the LORD. 'For as the heavens are higher than the earth, so are My ways higher than your ways, and My thoughts than your thoughts.'"

This verse could explain why so many Christians today are missing God's calling for their lives. Without realizing it, we expect God to func-tion out of our logic. God will not. Yes, God does speak—and He speaks clearly, in His own way and time. He often chooses the "ordinary" in life and allows us to more clearly see the difference His presence makes. It is because God chooses to use the ordinary to do extraordinary things that His works are remembered to the end of time, becoming an encourage-ment to all who obey Him.

Without realizing it, we expect God to function out of our logic. God will not. Yes, God does speak—and He speaks clearly, in His own way and time.

Let's take a look at some scriptural examples of how God uniquely encounters His people in the Old Testament Scripture:

- **Moses** encountered the Lord on a very ordinary day of his life. Yet when he saw God's activity on the mountain, he turned aside and met God through a burning bush (Exod. 3).

- **Samuel** was just a boy when God encountered his life. He heard an audible voice calling to him, and when Samuel responded to God's voice, God revealed His ways to him (1 Sam. 3).

- **David**, who tended his father's sheep, was chosen by God and anointed by God's servant Samuel to be the leader and king of Israel. After his anointing, "the Spirit of the LORD came upon David from that day forward" (1 Sam. 16:13).

- **Isaiah** "saw the Lord sitting on a throne, high and lifted up" (Isa. 6:1). God revealed all His majesty to Isaiah and then purified Isaiah's mouth with a live coal, cleansing him to be his prophet.

Then in the New Testament, God continues to reveal Himself in unique ways to individuals:

- **Joseph**, Jesus' earthly father, encountered the Lord through dreams. Not only was he instructed through his dreams about his future wife, but also how to protect Jesus and where to live.

- **The disciples** were also going about their daily lives when Jesus encountered them personally. They were offered a choice to continue on their chosen path or follow Him.

- **Paul**'s encounter with the Lord on the road near Damascus was sudden. The Lord surrounded Paul with a "bright light from heaven" (Acts 22:6 NIV) and after hearing what the Lord had to say, he was blinded. It is interesting that, although Paul was not alone, he was the only one who experienced and understood this encounter with the Lord (Acts 9:1–9).

> As he [Saul] journeyed he came near Damascus, and
> suddenly a light shone around him from heaven. Then
> he fell to the ground, and heard a voice saying to him,
> "Saul, Saul, why are you persecuting Me?" And he said,
> "Who are you, Lord?" Then the Lord said, "I am Jesus,
> whom you are persecuting. It is hard for you to kick
> against the goads." So he, trembling and astonished,
> said, "Lord, what do You want me to do?" Then the
> Lord said to him, "Arise and go into the city, and you
> will be told what you must do." And the men who
> journeyed with him stood speechless, hearing a voice
> but seeing no one. (Acts 9:3–7)

This is just a small sample of people whose lives God touched with a special encounter. Every experience was unique for each person. As in all encounters, God had a special plan and message for that person. Each person knew that God had encountered him in a special way and made the choice to follow the Lord in obedience.

Mary's encounter with the Lord was also uniquely tailored for her, revealing God's special plan for her life. The archangel, Gabriel, was God's chosen messenger sent to bring the "glad tidings" to Mary. It is also important to remember that God sent this same angel to Zacharias to announce the blessing of his son, John, who would later prepare the way for the Lord. Did this make Mary's encounter any less unique? No. In fact, it is easy to see how much the Lord cared for Mary. By giving her relatives a similar experience, she was not only able to receive affirmation from them, but was also able to share the encounter completely and be understood! How difficult and lonely it would have been for her without this confirmation of the Lord's words.

Looking at Mary from our perspective, she was young and was having to deal with incredible changes in her life. She was engaged to be married while dealing with this revelation from God's angel. Believing God's message telling her why she was pregnant and living with the whispers and gossip of all those around her would not have been an easy experience. It must have been both a blessing and relief that the Lord provided Elizabeth and Zacharias a similar experience to help encourage her in the faith! Gabriel was very specific: "Now indeed, Elizabeth your relative has also conceived a son in her old age; and this is now the sixth month for her who was called barren. For with God nothing will be impossible" (Luke 1:36–37). Mary's response on hearing this was immediate faith and obedience.

And the Angel of the LORD appeared to him in a flame of fire from the midst of a bush. So he looked, and behold, the bush was burning with fire, but the bush was not consumed. Then Moses said, "I will now turn aside and see this great sight, why the bush does not burn." So when the LORD saw that he turned aside to look, God called to him from the midst of the bush and said, "Moses, Moses!" And he said, "Here I am." (Exod. 3:2–4)

God's ways are not man's ways! He is thorough and leaves nothing incomplete. There is no detail that escapes His attention or fact that He's forgotten. He prepared the lives of Zacharias and Elizabeth to be a godly influence for Mary. He gave them similar experiences to confirm Mary's heart and faith. He gave her a refuge from the destructive gossip that she would experience in her hometown. He also prepared Joseph to accept Mary as his wife. By law, Joseph could have had her stoned. Being a just man, he was just going to "put her away quietly," or divorce himself from the betrothal agreement. The Lord intervened by sending an angel to him as well, preparing Joseph for the great responsibility of being Jesus' earthly father. Joseph's response also was immediate, and he was obedient to all God revealed to him.

Isn't it wonderful to know that when you have a special encounter with the Lord, it's in His perfect timing, it is uniquely for you, and every detail is already in place just waiting on your obedience!

It is sometimes easy for us to forget that when God does come to us, what He says will not only affect our lives but all those around us. God's announcement to Mary had a ripple effect that has been felt throughout history. It is no different when He encounters our lives today. When God chooses to bless us by allowing us to experience Him, there is always something special that He is about to do. There is always a "bigger picture" that we cannot see.

Learning to Listen
by Linda Hokit

I accepted Christ as Savior when I was seven years old, but I never understood what it meant to put my life in God's hands as Lord until the night I nearly died while driving.

I had just been appointed to serve as a short-term missionary in Vancouver, British Columbia, Canada, during the Expo '86 World's Fair. I was very excited because I had seen God's hand on the entire process. I was also looking forward to the drive south from my home in Anchorage, Alaska, on the famed Alcan Highway. I hoped it would be a nice relaxing vacation, since I planned to make the trip alone.

Friends were worried about my travel plans, but car travel was comfortable for me. I grew up in the 1960s and '70s when most families traveled by car. Plus, I had already run the wheels off two cars traveling by myself. Finally, my family traveled the Alcan when we moved to Alaska from California. I even remember my father letting air out of the tires on our station wagon so we could gain traction going over a snowy mountain pass as he drove between poles that marked the depth of the snow on the side of the road.

I remember the Canadian Mounty looking at our license plate as he strolled over to our car. He stuck his head in the window and said, "Welcome, Mr. Hokit. Another fifteen minutes and we would have come to find you." At age ten I thought it was cool that the Mounty knew my dad's name. Now at twenty-eight years old, as I again crossed the border, I remembered that I was going to serve the Lord in the country where the people looked out for me. Soon I would be looking out for them as well.

So, I had no fear traveling alone for a couple thousand miles, only a healthy respect for what could happen. Then one night I drove straight into a blizzard, and there was no way out! All of a sudden I heard a voice say, "Stop!" It nearly scared me to death because you don't stop in a blizzard, but you don't normally hear voices either. So I stopped. I opened the car door, and I realized there was a cliff. I had been driving on the wrong side of the road! A few more feet and I would have been on my way to heaven!

I pulled over to the right side of the road and wept. I prayed and thanked God for saving me, asked Him to keep cars from banging into me until I could carry on, and asked that He take me safely down the road to my destination. As I pulled out, the snow parted like the Red Sea! I drove like that for another half hour and then just as quickly as the snow came, it stopped.

Thankfully, God gave me another couple of days to ponder all that I had experienced before I arrived on the mission field. The folks in Vancouver probably will never know what a transformed person they received because of all I learned. I learned to hear and obey God's voice. I learned that God could take care of my life better than I could. I learned that wherever God leads I could go. I also learned that with God, there is always more to learn, no matter how many times you've been down the same road.

We have both known Linda for twenty years. We didn't know all that God had done before she arrived in Vancouver, but she certainly came with a heart to serve her Lord. We have seen her strive to always give her best in all that she does, faithfully giving witness to the love of Jesus. She has been involved in several different types of ministry, including Expo '86, Calgary's winter Olympics, and Stone Mountain Ministries in Georgia, and she is currently involved in mission work in her home state of Alaska.

GOD'S PURPOSE IN USING US

Little did I (Henry) know the extent to which God would choose to use my life to affect the lives of others. Beginning with ordinary things to do with God's people, God kept adding to the number and nature of the people He would let me influence. Today, I touch ambassadors at the United Nations, people who come to the Cove (Billy Graham's training center), top Christian CEOs of major companies in America, the military, marketplace ministries, college students, and many other peoples around the world. And it continues to increase. When God entrusts aspects of His Kingdom to those He chooses, it is so "open-ended." God let me speak at the Cove, which led to the opportunity to meet ambassadors at the U.N.

As I spoke with several people individually, many have invited me to come to their country, meet with their president, and be available to touch their nation redemptively. This is now leading me to minister in countries like South Africa. Once there, I am being invited to touch many other countries through them, even the African continent—and maybe, with the world focused on Africa, if revival comes there, to minister to the world. This is just like God. God wants to "touch a world" through any life wholly available to Him.

GOD LOOKS FOR THE LOYAL HEART

The big question is, why did God choose these people (Mary, Joseph, Zacharias, and Elizabeth) in particular to use in such mighty ways? We know that God comes uniquely and individually to a person, giving opportunities to be involved in His work and to grow deeper in relationship with Him. God never comes to us without having everything we need already in place, with every detail already cared for. At the beginning of this chapter, we quoted 1 Samuel 16:7: "Do not look at his appearance or at his physical stature, because I have refused him. For the LORD does not see as man sees; for man looks at the outward appearance, but the LORD looks at the heart."

This passage is referring to David's older brother. David and his brothers were raised in the same house, had the same genetics, same father, and were probably even similar in appearance! Yet God had refused all of the older ones in favor of the youngest and least likely. God's ways are not man's ways. Samuel would have chosen the older brother who looked the part of a king. God's response instead was to choose the one whose heart was ready to obey and serve Him. It was David's heart that God saw, and it is always the heart God is looking for. "For the eyes of the LORD run to and fro throughout the whole earth, to show Himself strong on behalf of those whose heart is loyal to Him" (2 Chron. 16:9).

God's plans for redemption could not, or would not, have been planned by man. The ways of God will always require faith. The Scripture even tells us that "without faith it is impossible to please Him" (Heb. 11:6). So different are the ways of God from ours that it is only through faith that we could recognize, believe, and trust Him, as Mary did.

God's ways will often surprise those He chooses and calls. He seems to drop into our everyday lives, giving us an opportunity to be a part of His work. There doesn't have to be a "big event" for God to speak to us. We must only have faith to know and recognize when it is God. He reads our hearts and looks at our character to see if He can trust us with eternal matters. To God, there is too much at stake to trust eternity to those of us who are unwilling to yield every part of our lives to Him.

Often, Christians desire to be used of God, but they do not have the prerequisites that are required for the encounter. They have not committed their lives fully to the Lord or readied their hearts to be obedient. Mary had a faith already in place for God to see. She had prepared her heart to be obedient, and God knew that He could entrust His Son into her care and that she would respond immediately to His timing in history.

Often, Christians desire to be used of God, but they do not have the prerequisites that are required for the encounter. They have not committed their lives fully to the Lord or readied their hearts to be obedient.

There are things we can do to prepare our hearts for the Lord: Love Him and seek after Him! Spend time in His Word and in prayer. Psalm 24:4–5 tells us, "He who has clean hands and a pure heart, who has not lifted up his soul to an idol, nor sworn deceitfully. He shall receive blessing from the LORD, and righteousness from the God of his salvation."

Don't allow sin a place in your life. Daily confess your sin or your lack of obedience to the Lord's commands. Ask the Lord to create a clean heart in you (Ps. 51:10) so that there is nothing in your life that would hinder Him from having immediate and complete access to you.

When He does come to you, know that the timing is perfect and every detail has already been thought through. Trust Him! He has a bigger picture than you do, and He is revealing His will so that you can have the opportunity to do something that no one else can do. Our responsibility is to make sure that our hearts are always prepared and pure before the Lord. A wholly yielded life, like Mary's, is what God is looking for.

QUESTIONS FOR STUDY AND RESPONSE

1. God chooses to speak uniquely to every individual. The timing, the manner, the method, and the message are God's way of relating in a real and personal way to us individually. In your desire to experience God in your life, have you ever tried to limit Him in how He wants to speak to you?

2. The people mentioned in this chapter all experienced the Lord in a powerful and individual way—and it changed their lives forever! Has God ever done something in your life that you know, beyond a shadow of a doubt, that it was Him calling or speaking to you? How did you respond? If you adjusted your life to obey the Lord, how did you see God work through your life? If you did not obey, have you asked God to forgive and heal your life?

3. God never leaves anything to chance when He is working. There is no detail that He has overlooked or left undone. Looking through the heritage listed for Jesus, it is clear that God began preparations before the beginning of man! Looking through your life, can you see that God has prepared your life in a special way? Are there some "loose ends" that you see Him tying up to free you for something special?

4. When God does encounter your life, it will have an effect on all those around you—your family in particular. Have you allowed others to deter you from following God's call on your life? Or has your family shared in God's blessing because of your obedience?

CHAPTER 7

MARY'S RESPONSE TO THE LORD

Behold the maidservant of the Lord!
Let it be to me according to your word.
—LUKE 1:38

WHEN GOD SPEAKS TO US, there are many possible ways to respond. Some of us do not know how to hear God's voice, often completely missing when He is speaking. Since we have not heard His voice, we do not know to respond. Some respond to the Lord with outright rebellion, rejecting the calling from God through disobedience to His words. With unbelief in their hearts, others "wrestle" with what God has revealed to them, taking precious time to sort through all that God has said. Some of us know what God has called us to do, yet we allow circumstances to quench what God had planned for our lives. Another group of us has already committed our ways to the Lord and is ready and willing to serve regardless of what God tells us. Mary was one who knew that God was God—and she was not—and her response revealed this. Her response, put in a song (Luke 1:46–55), is amazing coming from a teenage girl!

❧❧❧❧❧❧❧❧❧❧❧❧❧❧❧❧❧❧❧❧❧❧❧❧❧❧❧❧

And Jesus, walking by the Sea of Galilee, saw two brothers, Simon called Peter, and Andrew his brother, casting a net into the sea; for they were fishermen. Then He said to them, "Follow Me, and I will make you fishers of men." They immediately left their nets and followed Him. Going on from there, He saw two other brothers, James the son of Zebedee, and John his brother, in the boat with Zebedee their father, mending their nets. He called them, and immediately they left the boat and their father, and followed Him. (Matt. 4:18–22)

❧❧❧❧❧❧❧❧❧❧❧❧❧❧❧❧❧❧❧❧❧❧❧❧❧❧❧❧

Mary's response to Gabriel's announcement of God's favor was clearly seen in the song she sang while with Elizabeth and Zacharias. Mary had received a strong affirmation for all she had experienced from Elizabeth, her older cousin who was to give birth in her old age to John the Baptist. Elizabeth announced to Mary, "As soon as the voice of your greeting sounded in my ears, the babe leaped in my womb for joy. Blessed is she who believed, for there will be a fulfillment of those things which were told her from the Lord" (Luke 1:44–45).

With such assurance coming to her from her godly and trusted cousin, Mary broke out into a song. This song has become known as "the Magnificat." It is interesting that Mary's song was in the same tradition as the song of Hannah (1 Sam. 2:1–10) and also Moses' (Exod. 15:1–18) and Miriam's (Exod. 15:21) songs, as they also marveled over God's goodness to them through songs of praise and worship.

Remembering God's works through song was so important to God that He commanded Moses to write a song for all Israel to sing of His great works on their behalf (Deut. 31:19). The people needed to always remember and recount God's goodness, His mighty acts and works, and His provision for His people. They were sung as reminders of the greatness of the God who had chosen them and blessed them.[1] Mary also needed to remember and recount God's miraculous encounter with her, and she may have sung her song for the rest of her life. The song was to remind her of God's favor on her and the need for obedience, which would allow God to fulfill His purposes through her. Here is Mary's song from Luke 1:46–55:

> My soul magnifies the Lord,
> And my spirit has rejoiced in God my Savior.
> For He has regarded the lowly state of His maidservant;
> For behold, henceforth all generations will call me blessed.
> For He who is mighty has done great things for me,
> And holy is His name.
> And His mercy is on those who fear Him
> From generation to generation.
> He has shown strength with His arm;
> He has scattered the proud in the imagination of their hearts.
> He has put down the mighty from their thrones,
> And exalted the lowly.
> He has filled the hungry with good things,
> And the rich He has sent away empty.
> He has helped His servant Israel,
> In remembrance of His mercy,
> As He spoke to our fathers,
> To Abraham and to his seed forever.

Mary begins her song, as do many others in the Scripture, by declaring that her soul magnifies the Lord. The word *magnifies* also tells us that this is not just a one-time experience, but a continual act from Mary's heart.[2] From the depth of her being she placed the greatness of her God before all others and worshipped Him alone.

In her song, she also acknowledged that she, like everyone else, was a sinner and in need of a Savior. She went further in verse 47 and bore witness of how her spirit rejoiced—and this joy was because God was *her* Savior. She acknowledges her "lowly estate" as God's maidservant. One interpretation is that He has noticed His servant in her humble station.[3] She understood what God had said in Isaiah 57:15, "For thus says the High and Lofty One who inhabits eternity, whose name is Holy: 'I dwell in the high and holy place, with him who has a contrite and humble spirit.'"

Mary had a deep humbleness that her God would choose her! She knew from Hebrew history of God's covenant with the people, that anyone God chose would be honored by all succeeding generations. And Mary knew that all this would be because "He who is mighty has done great things for me" (Luke 1:49). This fact would carry her over the painful and demanding coming years, and she would sing about this as her reminder.

Mary was overwhelmed that the God who had chosen her was holy. This would cause her to tremble in His presence and at His words to her. Mary was aware of God's mercy on her and on all "who fear Him," and that this mercy was for every generation.

A Spiritual Marker in My Life
by Patricia Owens

My husband, Ron, had made a new friend. This man, he told me, was gifted. He had some wonderful tunes and could write some fine song lyrics, but he had no musical training. He was looking for someone to write down his melodies and then write piano accompaniments for them. There was one particular song that he was anxious to get on paper. "So," Ron said, "I volunteered you!"

My initial response was of dismay, because although I was a music school graduate, I had never attempted anything like that and felt very much put on the spot. Nevertheless, a time was set up for him to come to our house for me to have the opportunity to hear his melody and song lyrics—a very pleasant secular song idea. With some fretting and with many reasons to use an eraser, I began working with his material the next day. To my surprise, there was some pleasure involved in the creative effort, but also a good bit of stress. What if he didn't like it after all my work? But he did like it— a lot! In fact, he liked it so much that he talked me into trying to set another of his songs.

The experience of doing the first one had shown me that I enjoyed the part of conceiving the musical ideas for the accompaniment but didn't enjoy having to think out all that was involved in putting those notes on paper—that was *work*! By the time the second song was completed, and he seemed enthusiastic about the result, I found myself with a question that I feel the Holy Spirit prompted me to pray. It was simply, "Lord, would You ever want to give me a song?"

Two or three days later I woke about 2:00 AM and realized that going over and over in my mind were music and words. I don't like getting up in the middle of the night and usually would have just rolled over and gone back to sleep. But I had never experienced anything like this before, and I remembered what I had asked the Lord. I got up and quietly went into another room and sketched out the music and the words so that I would not forget them. "Reach out, reach out and touch Jesus. Reach out, reach out and touch Jesus! In

faith reach out and touch Jesus. You'll find all you need in Him."
They proved to be the refrain of my first published song, and more
important, the beginnings of something that God would allow Ron
and me to do together in our ministry—collaborating on writing
songs. I could never have dreamed at that time that God would later
use our writing songs together as a means of sharing Christ in places
as far away as Russia. I believe that one simple response to the Lord in
the middle of the night and the writing of that first song opened my
heart to trusting Him for larger things.

THIS IS WHAT I ASK, LORD

This is what I ask, Lord, this is what I need,
A fresh new look at You and an honest look at me.
Though the looking shows me things I do not like to see,
This is what I ask, Lord, this is what I need.

---

*Patricia and her husband, Ron, worked closely with me (Henry) for
eleven years. I still interact in revival conferences with them both. One of
the reasons we asked Patricia about a moment in her life was because of
the uniqueness of God's presence through music. Her heart to both sing
and play the piano has deeply touched my life and the ministry as we
have served together.*

*I (Carrie) have watched Patricia through the years, and one thing
that has touched me time and again is how she does the "little" things.
She is the glue that holds everything together! She is always sensitive to
the Lord's leading while she's playing and creates a beautiful atmosphere*

for people to respond to the Lord. She always took time to encourage me and has always been a wonderful example of how God can use a musician to reach others for Himself.

"FEAR AND TREMBLING" IN GOD'S PRESENCE

Fear and trembling are often linked in the Scriptures to describe the reverence we should have for the Lord. These characteristics are what Paul urged for every Christian. Philippians 2:12–13 says, "Work out your own salvation with fear and trembling; for it is God who works in you both to will and to do for His good pleasure."

There was a "trembling" in Mary at her first encounter with God through Gabriel. She had a simplicity and transparent honesty as she lived out her life. At every point in her life, she had wonder and awe, being amazed at all God was doing. This sense of awe continued in her as Jesus grew. As He began His ministry, she seems to have remained this way. This "trembling" was not always pleasant or joyful, but often fearful and full of pain. Standing before the cross where her Son was being mercilessly put to death must have climaxed her "trembling." She was faithfully seeking to understand how God was working in her and her Son, causing her to trust and enabling her to do it.

Encounters with God ought to be lived out with fear and trembling, because God is present and at work. Through Jeremiah, God said, "Do you not fear Me? . . . Will you not tremble at My presence . . . ?" (Jer. 5:22).

It seems that today we have lost the trembling in God's presence, and this has led to disobedience rather than faith as Mary had lived. Have we lost the wonder of standing in nature before God as Creator? Have we lost the wonder of holding a newborn child? What about the wonder of being present when a person's soul is saved and God transfers him before our eyes from the "power of darkness . . . into the kingdom of the Son of His love" (Col. 1:13)? We must always be aware of who God is, and never take His presence or His blessing lightly. Our obedience to the commands of the Lord will be affected by our awe of Him.

AWE IN GOD'S PRESENCE

I (Henry) spoke to my third son, Mel, who pastors a church in Cochrane, Albert, Canada. I could sense the awe and wonder in his voice as he described leading two adults to the Lord recently. "What an awesome work of God," as he described it. I wish I could have been there with him as God was working in their lives. I pray I never lose the "trembling" as I work out into every corner of my life the greatness of God's salvation that He is working in me.

In her song, Mary continues to recount the historical and specific deeds of God, expressed faithfully to His people. She extolled against the proud, the mighty on their thrones, and the rich. She knew God's record for "exalting the lowly, filling the hungry with good things, and helping His servant Israel"—all by His mercy. She was also speaking to the future and to God fulfilling His promises to His people. The Lord would bring justice to the land and to her people!

Finally, Mary remembered how God had "spoken" to her fathers, to Abraham and his seed, and that God would "speak forever"—even to her, His lowly maidservant. This record of God's specific activity on behalf of those He chooses would be her strength and shield for the rest of her life.

A BLESSED PIANO

It was in our first year as missionaries to Germany that God reminded me of the importance of worship through song. Wendell and I (Carrie) were studying German every day in school and also attending a local German Baptist church. After about eight months, I realized that I was struggling to encounter the Lord. I was growing frustrated with a difficult language and did not feel a peace in my life. What a terrible discovery for a missionary in her first year!

I quickly went before the Lord and came to the understanding that a huge part of my life was missing since I came to Germany. Worship! I had been trained most of my life in piano, had played for several churches throughout the years, and had sung in several different choirs. Not having the outlet of playing piano or an understanding for several months of what we were singing in church struck a huge blow to my spirit. My husband started searching for a way to get a piano, and although it took a great sacrifice, we were able to buy one a month later.

Everything about my life completely turned around! Where earlier there was drudgery, there now was joy; where there was frustration, there now was peace. I am so grateful that God provided me the blessing of having a piano. I now know that even without one, I must always remember all that God has done for me through song.

Without the remembrance of God's greatness in our lives, we can be overwhelmed by circumstances and trials—but when our heart sings of God's faithfulness, love, mercy, truth, and justice, there is nothing to stop us from seeing God accomplish all that He intends and becoming that blessing to all those around us. David's verses in Psalms have always held great meaning for my life. He says:

> I waited patiently for the LORD; and He inclined to me, and heard my cry. He also brought me up out of a horrible pit, out of the miry clay, and set my feet upon a rock, and established my steps. He has put a new song in my mouth—praise to our God; many will see it and fear, and will trust in the LORD. (Ps. 40:1–3)

HENRY'S SONG

As I (Henry) mentioned earlier in this chapter, one of the great joys of my life has been when God linked my life with Ron and Patricia Owens, both skilled musical performers and composers. During the eleven years we served together, we shared in some of the most significant encounters with God. And as we experienced God, Ron and Patricia would write these experiences into songs, which I sing to this day. They wrote about experiencing God, about revival and spiritual awakening, the goodness of God, and the cost in following God.[4]

God often gives those He chooses a song to be sung throughout their lives, to encourage them and keep them faithful to their God-given calling. Many throughout history, including in our day, have written songs like this from their encounters with God. Most of the great and lasting and influential hymns that we sing today are expressions of personal growth and testimony of the greatness of God's activity in people's lives! My favorite hymn, which has given me strength while going through very difficult times, is "It is Well with My Soul." Although the words and music are very beautiful, it's the story behind the words that encourages me to trust in the Lord and His goodness.

GOD'S MUSICIANS

Horatio G. Spafford knew both loss and devastation in his life. He was an attorney who lost a fortune in the great Chicago fire of 1871, yet he spent himself to help people recover from the tragedy. During this same time, his four-year-old son was lost to scarlet fever. To give his family some relief from the grief and constant work, he decided to take his wife and daughters to Europe to be physically and spiritually refreshed. He was detained in New York but decided to send his family ahead of him on the luxury liner *Ville du Havre*.

Without warning one night, the liner collided with an iron sailing vessel, killing 226 people—including Horatio's four daughters. His wife survived, sending back a telegram, "Saved alone." He quickly set sail to join his wife, and when he reached the area where the liner went down, he wrote, "It is well; the will of God be done." The song lyrics were written after this powerful expression of trust and peace that can be only found in the Lord.[5]

IT IS WELL WITH MY SOUL (1873)

When peace, like a river, attendeth my way,
When sorrows, like sea billows roll;
Whatever my lot, Thou hast taught me to say,
"It is well, it is well with my soul."

My sin, O the bliss of this glorious tho't,
My sin not in part but the whole
Is nailed to the cross and I bear it no more
Praise the Lord, Praise the Lord, O my soul!

O Lord, haste the day when my faith shall be sight,
The clouds be rolled back as a scroll;
The trump shall resound and the Lord shall descend
"Even so" it is well with my soul.

It is well, it is well, it is well, it is well with my soul.

One of the best loved writers of her day was Fanny Crosby. She had an amazing gift of hearing any written melody and matching it with words that were in her heart. "Blessed Assurance, Jesus Is Mine" came out of simply hearing the tune her friend had composed.[6] Her love of people was expressed so clearly through "Rescue the Perishing, Care for the Dying" as she dedicated much of her life to the Manhattan slums and rescue missions.[7] Yet her life testimony was best expressed through the hymn, "All the Way My Savior Leads Me," as Fanny was almost totally blind. She so clearly felt her Savior leading her through all aspects of her life, caring for her in every way. Although her blindness was most likely caused by an inept doctor in her infancy, she was often found to say that her blindness was the best thing that ever happened because God granted her "soul-vision."[8] Hear her story through her words.

ALL THE WAY MY SAVIOR LEADS ME (1875)

All the way my Savior leads me; what have I to ask beside?
Can I doubt His tender mercy, who thro' life has been my guide?
Heavenly peace, divinest comfort, here by faith in Him to dwell!
For I know, whate'er befall me, Jesus doeth all things well.

All the way my Savior leads me, cheers each winding path I tread,
Gives me grace for ev'ry trial, feeds me with the living bread.
Tho' my weary steps may falter, and my soul athirst may be,
Gushing from the Rock before me, Lo! A spring of joy I see.

All the way my Savior leads me, O, the fullness of His love!
Perfect rest to me is promised in my Father's house above.
When my spirit, clothed immortal, wings its flight to realms of day,
This my song thro' endless ages: Jesus led me all the way.

There were many different ways in which Mary could have responded to this encounter from the Lord. After her initial questions about how it would be possible, she immediately accepted the proclamation and never turned away from all that God intended for her life. Mary's Magnificat is a pure example of her love for her Lord. She praised her Lord, declaring His Lordship over her life and her devotion to Him. She was thankful and humbled that her Lord would choose to work through her. She sang of His faithfulness to His people, of His mighty deeds in the past, and how He would restore justice for His people.

Mary's response was also in reverence for the Lord. Her sense of fear and trembling came from her knowledge of who God is. Here was the Creator of the universe taking the time to involve her in His plan to redeem the lost world! When she realized this, her worship and praise were heartfelt, and this experience would continue to be remembered in her heart as she faced many trials and much pain.

As Jesus passed on from there, He saw a man named Matthew sitting at the tax office. And He said to him, "Follow Me." So he arose and followed Him. (Matt. 9:9)

When God interacts with our lives for a special purpose, it should be a time of great rejoicing! Our Creator has chosen us to reveal a part of His plan, and He allows us to be involved in His work. What a blessing! Our response should be similar to Mary's: praise and remembrance of who He is; a sense of awe, fear, and trembling that He would come to us; humility that He has chosen to work in our lives; thankfulness for what He has done and is going to do; obedience to do and complete His assigned mission.

We should also remember that when we sing praises to our Lord with our hearts full of love for Him, He will be honored in our lives. There is a direct link to how we express our love for Him through song and how we honor Him through our lives. Moses, Miriam, Hannah, David, Zacharias, Mary—these believers' songs could have easily been lost to us. Yet God chose to preserve them in Scripture as a testament to their love for Him. By the way, the Scripture does not tell us that only the musically talented can sing God's praises! God is always looking at the heart to determine if worship is acceptable in His sight. This is an important example for us today. As we sing of God's greatness and all His mighty works, others will clearly see the difference that He makes in our lives.

QUESTIONS FOR STUDY AND RESPONSE

1. Mary's heart was prepared to be obedient to whatever the Lord should ask of her. Does your heart respond immediately in obedience when you have an encounter with the Lord, or must you know the "who, where, what, why, and when"?

2. Mary's response in song clearly revealed her depth of understanding of how God has historically worked in Israel. Have you remembered God's faithfulness throughout the ages? Do you often remember His faithfulness in your life? Does His faithfulness cause you to be faithful to Him?

3. When we look at Mary's response to her encounter with the Lord, we can see the sense of awe and wonder that God would chose to use her. She understood who was sending the message to her through Gabriel—and trembled in His presence! Likewise, we are also exhorted to tremble in God's presence. When was the last time you stood before the Lord with "fear and trembling"? When have you felt that sense of awe that the God of the universe chose to come to your life?

4. Mary was so overcome with joy that she had to sing a song of God's greatness. When God comes to our lives, we should have that same joy. Have you ever had such a powerful encounter with the Lord that you had to sing His praise? Have you written your song?

5. The singing of hymns often brings us certain feelings or remembrances of situations or events. Singing hymns with an understanding of the composer's or author's circumstances can bring a deeper and more powerful awareness of the Lord and how He works in our lives. Do you have a favorite hymn that has spoken to you through times of difficulty? If you don't sing or have a musical favorite, how do you express your relationship with the Lord?

CHAPTER 8

GOD'S BIGGER PICTURE

*Just as He chose us in Him before the foundation of the world, that
we should be holy and without blame before Him in love, having
predestined us to adoption as sons by Jesus Christ to Himself,
according to the good pleasure of His will . . .*
—EPHESIANS 1:4–5

MY (CARRIE) FAMILY and I recently had the privilege of spending five
months in Cochrane, Alberta, working with the Canadian Southern
Baptist Seminary. It was an exciting and challenging time for Wendell
and me to be a part of God's work there. It was especially fun because my
husband had never had the opportunity to live in Canada, and one of my
wishes was for him to experience the Northern Lights (aurora borealis).
I had seen them often as a young person, and it was always a deeply moving experience.

Late one evening, two days before moving back to Georgia, I was
having some quiet time with the Lord on our back porch. After ten minutes, I noticed that it was getting lighter outside! I glanced over and saw
the beginnings of the Northern Lights.

I quickly woke my husband, and we stood together in the middle of a field watching the lights sweep across the sky. It was the most magnificent display I had ever seen! As we stood in awe of what I was considering my answer to prayer, I noticed very few people were outside enjoying the miracle. I wanted to call all my friends, yank them out of bed, and let them know what God was doing. I didn't want them to miss it. It was at that moment that God brought a deeper understanding to my heart. "You are disappointed that people are missing this display of lights. Yet I am working daily, changing hearts and lives. And just like people are missing this tonight, My people are also missing My activity in their lives and in those around them." What a heartbreaking revelation!

THE EFFECT OF MARY'S OBEDIENCE

Mary did not miss God's activity or His call on her life. She lived out her life in obedience to all that God revealed to her. What Mary could not understand or know in her lifetime was how her obedience affected all those around her and all those throughout the ages to come. It is so hard to see far beyond our time here on this earth. We may have read history books or tried to understand the revelation into the future, but there is no way for us to have an accurate assessment of the different ages. Yet God's perspective is eternity! God chooses all things and determines all things—from eternity and for eternity. God saw and knew Mary's life long before she was born. It was in eternity that God purposed redemption. He planned and purposed the when and the how. Therefore, Mary was chosen from eternity to be the earthly mother of Jesus. In God's *fullness of time* . . . God sent forth His Son, born of a woman, born under the law, to redeem those who were under the law" (Gal. 4:4–5, italics added). And God had eternity in mind when He did it. Through His Son, God

110

purposed that "He [Jesus] became the author of eternal salvation to all who obey Him" (Heb. 5:9).

Mary's life was therefore eternally in the mind, heart, and activity of God. Her life and call were not accidental, nor were they incidental. And no one's life should be seen from any other perspective. Every one of us has been eternally purposed and planned, and in God's fullness of time is brought into this world. Then God encounters us to reveal His eternal purposes. This dimension places not only infinite value on our lives but gives all who obey eternal significance. We, like Mary, can also impact eternity! Jesus said, "Do not lay up for yourselves treasures on earth . . . but lay up for yourselves treasures in heaven" (Matt. 6:19–20).

From God's perspective, Mary's life and ours have eternal significance. Though Mary knew the Scriptures, she could not see where she fit in to God's plan or activity. Neither can we! We read and know Scripture, but we can't always see or understand where we fit in to God's eternal purposes either.

There is no doubt that God's vision extends far beyond our comprehension. Sometimes we are so limited in our view of God's work because we have no way of knowing the scope of all God's activity without Him revealing it to us. We must understand that when God reveals Himself to us, He has a much bigger picture in mind. He has eternity in mind. When He comes to us in His perfect timing, He has something greater planned that we can't see.

This was certainly true in Mary's life. There was no way for her to know what God was doing in other people's lives and how they were going to be directly affected by her obedience. It is important to take a closer look at all those around the birth of Christ who were able to share in a special encounter with the Lord. We will also try to see how some of

God's people completely missed this opportunity, as well as one who sought to destroy what God was doing.

THE HEAVENLY HOSTS

And suddenly there was with the angel a multitude of the heavenly host praising God and saying: "Glory to God in the highest, and on earth peace, goodwill toward men!" (Luke 2:13–14)

The Amplified Bible has a beautifully descriptive translation that is helpful in shedding more light on this event:

Then suddenly there appeared with the angel an army of the troops of heaven (a heavenly knighthood), praising God and saying, "Glory to God in the highest [heaven], and on earth peace among men with whom He is well pleased [men of good will, of his favor]." (brackets in original)

These heavenly beings were not only aware of God's activity and plan to redeem the lost world, they were His messengers announcing the birth of the Son. How interesting that God would send His army to announce peace![1] While the world was slumbering or going about their business, all of heaven was singing praises to the Lord for sending His salvation! And make no mistake; all of heaven knew of Mary's obedience and faith in the Lord her God.

THE SHEPHERDS (LUKE 2:8–20)

So it was, when the angels had gone away from them into heaven, that the shepherds said to one another, "Let us now go to Bethlehem and see

this thing that has come to pass, which the Lord has made known to us."
(Luke 2:15)

There is a general consensus that these shepherds were most likely
tending the temple flocks that were used for the temple sacrifices. During
this time period, shepherding was a lowly position reserved for those who
knew no profitable trade. Leon Morris suggests that shepherds, as a class
of people, had bad reputations often linked with thieves as they moved
throughout the land. They were unable to observe the important religious ceremonial laws, which meant so much to the people, and their testimonies were deemed unreliable in the courts.[2]

Yet clearly, when God looked down on these humble shepherds, He
looked at their hearts and chose to miraculously share the good news of
Christ's birth with them! Why? To understand this, we must look to their
response and actions. Luke 2:15 tells us that they immediately traveled
to Bethlehem, believing what the Lord had revealed to them as truth.
They didn't respond with "let's go see if this is true"; they responded with
trust in the Lord and faith that these words were true. They knew that
the Lord had chosen to show them favor, and they "came with haste" to
see the child (v. 16). After the experience of meeting Jesus, they returned
rejoicing and praising God for all the things they had heard and seen,
telling everyone who would listen!

These shepherds must have been devout men who, with much free
time in the evenings under the stars, spent a great deal of time with the
Lord. It should be a great encouragement to us today to understand that
God doesn't concern Himself with power, type of job, money, status or
social class, race, perceived reputation, or any other factor that society
sees as important. He continuously looks at our hearts and our readiness
to obey His commands.

THE WISE MEN (MATT. 2:1–12)

And when they had come into the house, they saw the young Child with Mary His mother, and fell down and worshiped Him. (Matt. 2:11)

It is probably with great purpose that there is not much mentioned scripturally about the wise men from afar. Although there are traditions associated with them, including names and where they were from, the Bible does not take the focus away from the true meaning of the testimony—Jesus! What we do know is that these wise men, known as "Magi," were from a highly educated class of people who probably studied astrology and astronomy. "From the East" could have meant Persia, Arabia, or Mesopotamia, but this is uncertain.[3] They were wealthy and respected men who were allowed into Herod's inner courts and were granted an audience with the king. But why was this phenomenal story included in Matthew's gospel? There are several possible reasons worthy of note.

First, although these men were not of God's chosen race, they had been diligently searching the heavens for a sign of the coming King. They had been looking even for the smallest sign of a Savior and were willing to follow it until they found Him. Their hearts kept them on the path when all others would have given up. There is no way of knowing what they actually saw in the heavens, but only through divine guidance could they have come upon the house where Jesus was.[4] They immediately fell on their faces and worshiped the Lord with the best that they had to offer. This seems to be a divine principle that holds true throughout the Scriptures and to our day: When someone is truly searching for the Lord, God always provides a way to find Him![5]

When the wise men came into Jerusalem, they were probably disheartened that no one knew of the birth of the King. After they had inquired about the new King they were seeking, Matthew 2:3 says, "When Herod the king heard this, he was troubled, and all Jerusalem with him."

Why were these people "troubled" and not excited about the coming King? The wise men might have wondered how the people could not have known when they had seen the star from such a far distance. How could these people have missed such an important event when they themselves had traveled so far and given up so much for the journey? Yet even in the wise men's discouragement from the people in Jerusalem, they still looked up! Verse 10 says, "When they saw the star, they rejoiced with exceedingly great joy." They could have left grumbling with their heads down, missing the greatest blessing of their lives. But the Lord in His mercy again renewed His sign for them, helped them fulfill their heart's quest, and kept them safe from harm upon their return (vv. 9–12).

KING HEROD THE GREAT AND THE RELIGIOUS LEADERS

And he sent them [the wise men] to Bethlehem and said, "Go and search carefully for the young Child, and when you have found Him, bring back word to me, that I may come and worship Him also." (Matt. 2:8)

To list Herod among these great encounters with the Lord is difficult, yet his role in the early life of the baby Jesus is crucial. Because of the many historical records of Herod the Great, we have a large amount of information regarding his rule over the Jews. Initially during his reign, he was seen as crafty, as he was able to ingratiate himself to two different rulers to keep himself in power. He was also responsible for building many of the ancient cities and was credited for rebuilding the temple in Jerusalem.[6]

It didn't take long, however, for his power to corrupt him completely. After ruling as king from 37 B.C., his jealous and suspicious nature took control, and he began to assassinate and murder all those he suspected as wanting his throne.[7] He is known to have murdered his brother-in-law Aristobulus, a very popular high priest, in 35 B.C.[8] He subsequently killed his own wife and her mother, his two brothers-in-law, his firstborn son, many loyal courtiers, army officers, three hundred soldiers, and others.[9] Knowing this background, it is not hard to imagine how Herod would have responded to the inquiries from apparent royalty from the East about the new infant "king"! Herod's slaughter of the infants in Bethlehem is recorded in Matthew 2:16:

> Then Herod, when he saw that he was deceived by the wise men, was exceedingly angry; and he sent forth and put to death all the male children who were in Bethlehem and in all its districts, from two years old and under, according to the time which he had determined from the wise men.

What a terrible tragedy! Why did the wise men go to Herod and unknowingly instigate this turn of events? We do know that this event was foretold by Jeremiah (Jer. 31:15). This should have been an unmistakable and irrefutable sign to the chief priests and scribes that the Messiah had indeed been born. How could they have missed this one? Yet we know that they chose to ignore the Scriptures in favor of their traditions and belief that the Messiah would come the way they expected Him to. They could have been true spiritual leaders of God's people during the most exciting times in Christian history! Instead, they were condemned by Jesus Himself when He said to Jerusalem:

> If you had known, even you, especially in this your day, the things that make for your peace! But now they are hidden from your eyes. For days will come upon you when your enemies will build an embankment around you, surround you and close you in on every side, and level you,

and your children within you, to the ground; and they will not leave in you one stone upon another, because you did not know the time of your visitation. (Luke 19:42–44)

God's own people, to whom He had given the prophecies and all the promises of the Savior, completely missed the coming of Christ. His people were too busy with their own lives and problems to take the time to understand what God was saying to them. Instead, they were looking for what they wanted to see—a king who would free them politically and who would rebuild their kingdom—and Jesus condemned them for it.

Regardless of the plans of men, the Lord kept His purposes alive by protecting His Son. Because of Herod's evil heart, God warned Joseph through a dream to take his family and flee to Egypt (Matt. 2:13). This also fulfilled the prophecy recorded in Hosea 11:1. The chain of events could only have been foreseen and prepared for by the Lord.

SIMEON (LUKE 2:25–35)

Lord, now You are letting Your servant depart in peace, according to Your word; for my eyes have seen Your salvation which You have prepared before the face of all peoples, a light to bring revelation to the Gentiles, and the glory of Your people Israel. (Luke 2:29–32)

Simeon is described in Scripture as being a "just and devout" man who was "waiting for the Consolation of Israel" (Luke 2:25). He was seen as righteous or just with his fellow man, and considered devout in his relations to God.[10] He was waiting for the Messiah, the Deliverer, who would solve all of the oppression and problems that were facing the children of Israel.[11] The Heavenly Father chose this devout man to know and experience the young Savior for whom he was waiting. He recognized

Jesus as the Messiah and thanked the Lord for opening his eyes to this great blessing. Matthew also carefully records his specific words of prophecy to Mary, His mother: "Behold, this Child is destined for the fall and rising of many in Israel, and for a sign which will be spoken against (yes, a sword will pierce through your own soul also), that the thoughts of many hearts may be revealed" (Luke 2:34–35).

Already, God was preparing Mary's heart for the events to come in Jesus' life. What a special gift of compassion straight from her God! Even in the moment of our deepest pain, God knows and seeks to prepare our hearts. The Lord, through Simeon, was essentially helping Mary to understand that although she would face the ultimate pain for a mother, there was no other way to salvation.

It is often difficult to see God's bigger picture while we are in the midst of our pain. Yet, like Mary, we can trust that He loves and cares for us and will work out His will in the middle of our circumstances.

**It is often difficult to see God's bigger picture while we
are in the midst of our pain. Yet, like Mary, we can trust
that He loves and cares for us and will work out His will
in the middle of our circumstances.**

ANNA (LUKE 2:36–38)

And coming in that instant she gave thanks to the Lord, and spoke of Him
to all those who looked for redemption in Jerusalem. (Luke 2:38)

Anna (the name meaning "favor" or "grace") was also mentioned in Luke as having a special encounter with Jesus. In the Scripture, she is given the special distinction of being named a prophetess in an age where there had only been seven recognized.[12] After being married for seven years, she was widowed and lived out the rest of her life serving the Lord in the temple; the Scripture says for eighty-four years. She was a shining example of one of God's own, living a disciplined life of obedience and self-control.

Anna had prayed for years to be able to see God's faithfulness in sending the Redeemer, and Mary's obedience brought about the answer to Anna's fervent prayer. As a special blessing for her years of faithfulness, God allowed Anna to see her prayers answered in the form of Jesus. What a blessing it must have been to her! This story gives us a brief glimpse at the depth of compassion that God had for Anna, a widow.

Little did Mary realize that God's invitation to her and her obedience to Him would set in motion events in so many other people's lives.

At a Crossroads

by Marilyn Blackaby

I can't remember a time when I didn't want to be a missionary. From the time I spent in my church's Sunbeams and GA mission programs as a little girl, I always felt that God would use me in mission work—preferably in South America or somewhere that I could ride burros over the hills sharing about Jesus.

As I grew older, I continued to look toward missions and how I could be involved. We were living in California, and my husband was pastoring a church while working his way through his seminary degrees. We were able to see God do some wonderful things, changing many lives, but we still felt that pull into mission work. We went through the normal channels with the Foreign Mission Board (now known as the International Mission Board) and began the application process. Just as we were about to be appointed as career missionaries to Kenya, our oldest child became ill. We took him to several specialists, but no one could explain the cause of his condition. We were then turned down for the appointment and were told that until our son's health was controlled, we could not serve in foreign missions.

We were disappointed, but we focused on our son's health and the work that the Lord had already given us in the church. We knew that God was in control. It was only a few months after this that we were contacted by a man working in Canada. He was desperate. He thought that if Canadians didn't return to Canada to serve in the churches, there was the possibility of losing all the Southern Baptist work up there. There were actually more churches in Kenya than in Canada at that time! We prayed and felt that this was our mission field where God wanted us to serve.

Going from sunny California to the subzero snowy weather of Saskatchewan was difficult, yet I had always prepared for adventure. I knew that I'd have to deal with the cold, new schools for the kids, buying a completely different set of clothes without any money, working in a church that was initially smaller than our own family, having no financial stability or any agency that would underwrite our costs—this was a part of being a missionary! I was finally reaching my childhood dream! Then reality came crashing down.

Within the first year I was really struggling. All I did, literally, was fix three meals per day and spend much time cleaning the dishes (no dishwasher in those days), changing sheets, doing laundry (because everyone stayed at the pastor's house), vacuuming and cleaning floors from the snow and mud, and cleaning the house that had all the neighborhood children plus my four sons and one daughter playing. This was not the missionary life that I had always foreseen. This was not the life I had dreamed of as a little girl.

I could always talk to the Lord while I was doing work in the house, mostly washing dishes and vacuuming, because everyone disappears when there is work to do around the house. One day while I was vacuuming, I was praying and talking to the Lord. I told Him, "I always have wanted to be a missionary, and all I do is wash, clean, cook, vacuum, and do laundry all day long! Is this being a missionary?"

It was at this very difficult moment in my life that God encountered me in a very special and personal way. "Yes!" He told me. "This is your mission."

This freed me to look at my work differently. God opened my eyes and helped me see things through His perspective, and this was what He needed from me right then. It gave me a different vision of my work and completely changed my attitude. From then on, this was a ministry I had to all the people who visited my home, came for coffee, played in my yard, as well as to my own family that needed the love and care that only I could give.

As I look back, so many things in my life stemmed from this moment of obedience. My heart attitude was so important in my household. I did not always stay in this "cooking and cleaning" stage, but it was an important step in trusting the Lord with my mission for that time in my life. This encounter with the Lord set an important change in my heart that I never forgot, and I have often looked back on it when I needed some perspective.

It should come as no surprise that Marilynn/Mom was at the top of the list when it comes to women who've influenced our lives. We have both watched through the years as God continually encounters her life in special and powerful ways. There is no question to either of us that we would not be where we are without her love, dedication, and support.

God is always at work around us. He never sleeps. He never tires. He is actively working to bring people to Himself, and He has chosen to use us! God searches our hearts, knows when we are ready to experience Him, and chooses to reveal Himself and His will for our lives. What we must understand is that our lives are only a part of what God is doing. Often we as God's people can become so self-centered. We feel that, although God has come to us with how we can be involved in His plan, we can wait and wrestle with the decision of obedience. This is not an acceptable answer for the Lord. When the timing of our obedience is critical, can God trust us with the assignment? Yes, there is often a cost involved in the obedience—but what we don't understand is the cost of being disobedient.

Now the LORD had said to Abram: "Get out of your country, from your family and from your father's house, to a land that I will show you. I will make you a great nation; I will bless you and make your name great; and you shall be a blessing. I will bless those who bless you, and I will curse him who curses you, and in you all the families of the earth shall be blessed." (Gen. 12:1–3)

All of the people mentioned in this chapter had a moment of decision when God encountered them. The shepherds had to believe the message was true and leave their flocks, seek out the Child, humble themselves and worship Jesus, and then return home and share all that

God had revealed to them. The wise men sought after the Lord with great diligence, giving all they had (time, wealth, personal safety, and comforts) for this encounter with the King. Simeon and Anna had both lived a life devoted to the Lord, praying and waiting many years to see their Messiah—the only One who could save their people.

There were still others that, although they were highly educated in the Scriptures and knew all the factual information about the coming of the Messiah, missed the time of God's coming to them. The religious leaders and scribes understood the Scripture enough to tell Herod where the Savior would be born, and they knew from the wise men when the birth took place, yet they had no desire to find out the truth for themselves.

Like the wise men of old, many today are diligently searching for a Savior. They may not even know what they are looking for, but their hearts are yearning for more in life.

There are also others who do have knowledge of the Lord and what He could mean in their lives, but they have chosen to reject Him. Simeon's prophetic words are true to this day: "Behold, this Child is destined for the fall and rising of many in Israel, and for a sign which will be spoken against . . . that the thoughts of many hearts may be revealed" (Luke 2:34–35). God is in the "revealing hearts" business. Never think that you can deceive the Lord or hide your motivations or intentions.

Mary's life and her obedience to the Lord had a profound effect on all those around her, and the same is true for us today. Our obedience or disobedience has a wide effect that we may never know or see. Therefore, commit your ways to Him, and see how He will use you in His bigger picture to complete His purposes in our world today.

QUESTIONS FOR STUDY AND RESPONSE

1. God had worked through history, in the lives of many people, and in all the details surrounding the coming of Jesus. Like it was for Mary, it is impossible to see how God is shaping all the events around our lives to further His purposes. Have you ever been so caught up in your own situation that you have missed "the big picture" of God's work around you? If so, ask His forgiveness and that He would open your eyes to what He's doing in our day.

2. God entrusted the Good News of Jesus' birth to the shepherds, who immediately responded in obedience. Can God entrust the good news of Jesus to you?

3. Seeking and finding the Lord came at a great price to the wise men and all those around them. Are you willing to pay such a price to follow the Lord in obedience?

4. The temple leaders of Jesus' day were condemned for missing the time of God's coming to them. Are you trusting in your knowledge or tradition instead of the Scriptures and their revelation?

5. Anna and Simeon were recognized in the Scripture for their zeal and faithfulness to the Lord. It was after many years of faithfulness that God granted to them the blessing of seeing their Lord. God left this example for us so that we would be encouraged to remain

faithful to what we believe He has called us to do—especially in prayer. Is there something that you have been faithfully praying for through the years? Be encouraged that God will honor faithfulness— in His timing.

CHAPTER 9

THE STEWARDSHIP OF GOD'S SON

So when they had performed all things according to the law of the Lord, they returned to Galilee, to their own city, Nazareth. And the Child grew and became strong in spirit, filled with wisdom; and the grace of God was upon Him.

—LUKE 2:39–40

MY (HENRY) PARENTS didn't meet until after my father came home from World War I, so they were married later in life. At that time, my mother was a one-room-school teacher who believed in education and discipline. One of her favorite sayings was, "No child will ever drive me crazy. I may drive them crazy, but they will never drive me crazy!" She had a deep love for children and always sought to help them better themselves and learn personal responsibility. She encouraged a child's imagination and creativity and was faithful to share the love of Christ with every child.

As my father's job as a bank manager moved them to different locations, they continually helped to plant new churches wherever God placed them. Every Saturday evening, for several years, they would spend time cleaning up the beer bottles and other nasty paraphernalia at the local dancehall so they could hold church services the next day. Often it was only our family—but our family's relationship to the Lord was important enough for my parents to clean up that mess every week. My mother single-handedly started a Sunday afternoon Sunday school for all the children, which often had more than fifty children! Eventually, this led to a thriving, healthy church. But I watched my parents pay the cost for God to have an impact on the community.

My mother was always quoting Scripture. For every question, she knew a Scripture; for every problem, there was a favorite verse. She was faithful in prayer, and we often heard her praying out loud for her family, the missionaries, the troops during World War II, and God's work in our town. She encouraged us to give our best to the Lord and to always keep His paths before us.

To say that she was a powerful influence in my life would be an understatement! One of my most memorable impressions of my mother was when she faithfully sat down with my brothers and me and helped us to hear and understand what God was doing in our world and on the mission field. Missions was made personal as we heard from our mother's older sister and her husband, who were serving as missionaries in China. After many discussions and prayer times together, we suddenly began receiving news of the Shantung revival. We saw pictures of baptismal services of 100 to 150 people every time there was a meeting. What a wonderful sight!

These moments with my mother left a lasting impression on my heart about the ways and faithfulness of God. Later, when the Japanese invaded China, my aunt and uncle were imprisoned briefly, and my aunt's health took a turn for the worse. They returned home and miraculously avoided the massacre of missionaries that later occurred in China. I knew God to be faithful and always remembered my mother keeping God's ways and activity ever before us.

A MOTHER'S INFLUENCE

The relationship that we have with our mothers can be the most significant influence in our lives. Memories from early childhood can stay with us for a lifetime. This would also be true of Jesus' relationship with Mary. During this time period, it was the responsibility of the mother to train and instruct the child in his earlier years. Even though His religious training would have come from Joseph, it is likely that Jesus spent a great deal of time learning from His mother. She, therefore, would have had a great influence on Jesus' early years of life.

There are many silences in the Scripture on things that we would like to know and better understand. How was Mary treated by her family and in-laws while she was pregnant? Did she ever tell anyone other than Elizabeth and Zacharias about the proclamation? Did she ever discuss her experience with Jesus? What was Jesus like as a child? What was He like as a teenager? How did Jesus relate to His brothers? What was Mary's influence over her other children? We can only trust the Holy Spirit to help us understand the deeper dimensions of Jesus' early years. Yet in the silence, we can still find some deeper truths.

THE BIRTH OF CHRIST

It was in eternity that God purposed the time, the way, the manner, and the circumstances surrounding the birth of Jesus. From the beginning of time, God had planned every detail for His plan of salvation. But Mary could hardly have imagined the birth of her firstborn to come in such a manner. Much like today, young girls were brought up with certain expectations and dreams. In Mary's culture there was nothing more important than the birth of the firstborn son. There were often great celebrations and a recognition or rite of passage for a woman to be truly accepted into proper Jewish society. The birth of a child announced to all that God was expressing His favor on her family and marriage.

It is easy to look at Mary's life and think only of how blessed she was to have been chosen as God's vessel to bless all people. Indeed, her name will be known throughout time as the mother of Christ Jesus. Yet how did she have to adjust her life at such a tender age to accept God's assignment? What crisis of belief did she experience?

We are not told of the difficulties Mary endured before Joseph took her into his care. We could speculate about how she would have been treated as an unwed expectant mother or the disgrace that she and her family possibly endured. We do know that the birth of Mary's firstborn son was not the moment of elation that she had dreamed of. Instead of receiving the special care of her mother or a midwife, she was alone with her husband in a distant town. We are not told of anyone who gave Mary help in her great time of need. We are told of a stable or cave where the animals resided, of swaddling clothes, and of a manger. Mary was denied all of the comforts normally afforded to a new mother, especially for the firstborn male. How lonely it must have been when she should have been surrounded by the tenderest of care.

Yet she was not alone. God, out of His love for Mary, provided her with knowledge of the celebration taking place throughout the heavens.[1] The shepherds and wise men came to celebrate the birth of her Son, sharing their stories of their encounters with the Lord and confirming again to Mary her purpose in God's salvation plan. Although Mary went through this difficult time without her family, her Heavenly Father was watching over them, loving and protecting them from harm in the days to come.

A Precious Gift from God

by Gina Blackaby (married to Henry and Marilyn's son Mel)

Summer days were fast approaching, and our anticipated third child was almost here. Grandma (Marilynn) left early in the morning after her two-week visit waiting for this precious gift to arrive. Her last words were, "I know the minute I get on the plane this baby will come." We all laughed. The moment my husband, Mel, returned from the airport, our incredible journey began. With a mixture of deep joy and strong pain every five minutes, I knew it *was* time. We gazed at each other, laughed, and said, "Grandma was right." Our child was coming.

Sarah, our special gift from the Lord, was born at 11:17 that morning, June 9, 1998. What a bundle of joy, full of life and beauty! As parents of three children under the age of four, we trusted the Lord for guidance. God had given me three little ones, and I was so thrilled about what He had in store for our lives. We were always watching to see His hand. As we looked at our brown-haired, blue-eyed daughter, we didn't know that God would be directing our lives down a new path in the days ahead.

At five months of age, Sarah was sitting in the high chair, and I noticed that her tiny right hand was not functioning as well as her left hand. I also became aware that her right leg didn't kick as high as her left when she played in the bathtub. After seeing some weakness, we took her to our family doctor. He checked her reflexes and detected some neurological damage. He referred us to a pediatrician, and our appointment was scheduled for two months away. When I encountered this, my heart cried out to holy God! Could our precious little girl have anything wrong? As many thoughts raced through my mind, the Lord spoke so clearly, "Just trust Me as you always have. I am the same now, forever, and always!" He brought to the forefront of my mind the simple but clear Scripture I had memorized as a child, Proverbs 3:5–6, "Trust in the Lord with all your heart, and lean not on your own understanding; in all your ways acknowledge Him, and He shall direct your paths."

On my birthday, we finally sat in the pediatrician's office waiting for the result of the tests. The doctor came in the room. He sat down, looked us both in the eyes, and said, "Your daughter has cerebral palsy." Shock of the news froze my whole body as tears welled up in my eyes. I glanced at Mel for a reaction. The doctor explained that the brain had some degree of damage, and it was affecting her motor skills. How could I respond to such a diagnosis? Did I cause it? Could I have prevented it? All I knew was that as a teenager I had watched Jerry Lewis's telethons that raised money for CP children. I remembered severely disabled children that broke my heart. Was this what Sarah's future looked like? Then the Lord gently spoke to my heart and said, "Don't ponder all the what-ifs. Let Me show you all of who I am and promise to be!" Then He brought to the forefront of my mind His words, "And He is before all things, and in Him all things consist [hold together]" (Col. 1:17), and "Be anxious for nothing, but in everything by prayer and supplication, with thanksgiving, let your requests be made known to God; and the peace of God, which surpasses all understanding, will guard your hearts and minds through Christ Jesus" (Phil. 4:6–7).

I will never forget my thirty-third birthday. As my husband and I approached the car with Sarah in our arms, tears flowed down our cheeks, and our hearts were burdened by the news. She, however, had no idea, and her little smile illumined her face. She was still a promise from our Lord, and He gave her to us for a special reason!

We were in shock from the news, not remembering many details of the day. But what will always remain vivid is that special evening when we encountered God so personally. I remember my husband sitting in the armchair by the window with the stars shining bright, the Big Dipper clearly overhead. I sat at his feet with my elbow on his knee. There we pondered the things of God and how He had covered our lives with His love. He had blessed us with so much, and we had seen His mighty work in our lives and in our church. We recalled our pilgrimage with God and all the spiritual markers of walking with Him as a couple over the previous ten years. How could we question Almighty God who made the stars to shine, who is all in all, who formed our very being, who had been nothing less to us than all He said He would be and more? On and on we reminisced. What a powerful time, filled with the presence of God.

Then I considered the reality of the moment. *Will Sarah be able to crawl, walk, talk, drive, play the piano, ride a bike? But most importantly, will she be able to comprehend the things of God and know His great salvation? Where do I begin, Lord?* Then, as God always does, He spoke so tenderly and softly saying, "Do not worry about tomorrow, for tomorrow will worry about itself. Each day has enough trouble of its own" (Matt. 6:34–35 NIV). "Walk with Me, and take one day at a time. Trust Me with Sarah's life, and I will show you great and mighty things. Stay close to Me, and I will guide you each step of the way."

Immediately we went to our knees before the Father and asked for guidance to know His heart and His ways, knowing that in His presence we would find His peace and strength for the journey ahead. God filled my heart with anticipation as we knew we were right where He wanted us to be.

Peace like I had never known before filled my heart. I was now excited about this new journey to walk with the Lord. What was He going to do in and through our little Sarah, through us as a family, and through me as her mother? The Lord spoke softly, "Give her to Me and raise her to the glory of God."

The Lord prompted us to ask everyone we knew to pray with us. Sarah was put on prayer chains all over the world, and we received more than 350 cards and phone calls to say people were praying for our precious girl and our family. We were overwhelmed at God's goodness to our lives. We did all we knew to do physically for Sarah and enrolled her in many therapy classes. The Lord also provided a therapist who came to the home three times a week to teach me exercises to do with Sarah. It's been exciting to see God working in the lives of all He brings us in contact with.

God came to me in my darkest hour and made it a time of refreshing, rejoicing, and victory! He has been faithful, and Sarah's life has brought many others to a closer relationship with Him. God's hand is clearly on her life. Now at age seven, she is now walking, running, riding a two-wheeler, riding horses, learning to swim, and singing songs about Jesus. Our greatest joy, however, was to watch her write her testimony that she shared at her baptism. Someday she will shed her little body and spend eternity with us in heaven. God has met my every need and fulfilled every promise He made!

Before Gina became a member of our family, she came to Vancouver to serve as a semester missionary at Expo '86. Little did we know the impact she would later have! God has brought Gina through many challenging and difficult experiences and has created in her a heart of gold. Gina's friendship when I (Carrie) was a teen and the companionship we share now is and has always been a treasure. Mel and Gina, along with their

three children, live in Cochran, Alberta, where Mel is pastor at Bow Valley
Baptist Church.

THE STEWARDSHIP OF A CHILD

Mary's assignment did not stop at the birth of her Son. Now that the prophecy of Christ's birth was fulfilled, Mary had to raise the Child that God had entrusted to her for the next thirty years. What a daunting task! She also had to trust the Lord to equip her with the wisdom she needed to teach Jesus about God's truths and His ways. Giving birth to Jesus might later seem to be the easiest part.

The focus of the Scripture is *not* on Mary. Although Mary was an important person in the coming of the Messiah, the focus in the Scripture is on what God was doing through her life and the life of her Son. It would have been a somewhat simple task for any of the Gospel writers, Luke in particular, to have included a great deal more about Jesus' early years with His mother. Scholars believe that for Luke to have known the more detailed account of Jesus' birth, he must have spent a great deal of time questioning Mary about her experience.[2] Yet we have few details regarding Jesus' childhood experiences. Instead, the Scripture's main emphasis is on God's revelation to us about Himself and His ways. This emphasis keeps us from placing too great an importance on any one person and instead keeps our focus on God's activity in and through the life of Jesus.

OBEDIENCE TO THE LAW

There are several biblical references to Mary during these early years in Jesus' life. These passages clearly reveal her obedience to the Law, her integrity, and her love and concern for her Son. They also provide us with a godly example from whom we can gain a great deal of understanding for our own lives.

Joseph and Mary were faithful Jews who sought to follow the Old Testament requirements. Because of this fact, certain assumptions can be made regarding the spiritual development of Jesus.

In keeping with the Old Testament law, Luke 2:21 tells us that they had their child circumcised on the eighth day after His birth. This was not only an important act during this time period, but also a time of naming and dedicating the child to the Lord.[3] Once again, Mary's obedience is clear; she named her child "Jesus" as the angel had commanded (Luke 1:31; 2:21). Traditionally, this was a moment of great family celebration, for eight days after the birth also signaled that both mother and child would survive.[4] Yet the Gospel records have no mention of any family members attending this special time.

Mary and Joseph continued to express their obedience to the Scripture as they returned to Jerusalem to present their Son, Jesus, to the Lord. "Now when the days of her purification according to the law of Moses were completed, they brought Him to Jerusalem to present Him to the Lord (as it is written in the law of the Lord, 'Every male who opens the womb shall be called holy to the LORD')" (Luke 2:22–23).

After the initial ritual after the birth, it was important for Mary to make a sacrifice forty days after the birth.[5] Mary made her temple sacrifice according to the Law and offered two "turtle doves or pigeons" for her cleansing. Her sacrifice was that of the poor, for if she had had more money, she would have sacrificed a lamb.[6]

This firstborn son in the Jewish family was considered holy or "separated" unto the Lord.[7] This would especially be true of Jesus because of His kingly lineage recorded in both Matthew and Luke. God had seen to every detail of Jesus' birth, making sure that this sacrifice for our redemption was perfect and acceptable in every way.

JESUS' CHILDHOOD YEARS

We have no information of Jesus' childhood years, but we are told, "The Child grew and became strong in spirit, filled with wisdom; and the grace of God was upon Him" (Luke 2:40).

Jesus developed like any other child. He had to learn to walk, talk, interact with others, and obey His parents. He must have had bumps and bruises and challenges like the other children. The wording of the above passage is very important. It tells us that Jesus grew and *became* strong in spirit and filled with wisdom. He didn't start out with wisdom; He learned it![8] It is apparent that Joseph and Mary sought to obey all the commands of the Lord, and Jesus observed and became involved in their obedience. This should be such an encouragement to us, especially those of us who have been entrusted with a child. All children need guidance, instruction, and the tools to grow in knowledge of the Lord. They don't start out with wisdom and knowledge, but it must be methodically developed and built upon as they mature. Our responsibility, like Mary's, is to daily follow the commands of our Lord and to be that example our children need.

At every stage in Jesus' life, He was surrounded by the example of His parents. He observed the fullness of God's requirements for life. Jesus saw and understood obedience and how to express His love for God. So as He grew, He became "strong in spirit." His entire being was strengthened in His relationship with the Father. He was also "filled with wisdom." Exposed to the Scriptures, He was immersed in the wisdom of God, and He practiced obediently what He knew. When our hearts are set on obedience, we also will be immersed in the Scriptures and the grace of God, and we will be given the practical enabling to do the will of God. Jesus knew this early in His life, and Mary had a strong role to play in His understanding.

Mary would be a powerful individual in the life of Jesus, but she would decrease, and He would increase (see John 3:30). In the presence of Jesus, this is to always be true. Mary had to allow Jesus to become all that God intended, and in turn, begin letting go and allowing Him to make decisions. She chose to allow Jesus the freedom to grow and follow the Lord without seeking to interfere in what God was doing in His life. Mary was never shown as resisting this belief, but she did have to make some adjustments in her life. She could have been controlling or over-bearing, feeling the weight of her responsibility before the Lord. But because Mary allowed Jesus to mature and develop, we see her actions confirmed in the Scripture with Jesus growing in wisdom and grace.

Our next glimpse into the childhood of Jesus is at the age of twelve. His parents continued to walk in obedience with the scriptural laws, traveling to Jerusalem for the Feast of the Passover. After the days of the feast, they journeyed home, not knowing that Jesus was not with them. There is no way to know exactly why Jesus was left behind. It is possible that He did not know they were leaving, and He remained in the temple where He could be found. It was a custom during this time for the women and small children to travel at the head of the caravan while the men and older boys followed.[9] Each parent could have thought Jesus was with the other, but when they came together it was clear He was still in Jerusalem. After three long days of travel back to Jerusalem to find Jesus, Mary and Joseph finally found Him in the temple.

The temple had always been the center for instruction, and there was nothing out of the ordinary with a young boy willing to listen and learn from the group of scholars.[10] Jesus, who came from a smaller town with few good teachers, was clearly taking advantage of the time to learn all He could. When Mary and Joseph came upon Jesus, He was found rea-soning with the teachers in the temple. They "were astonished at His understanding and answers" to their questions (Luke 2:47). For a boy seeking knowledge, Jesus must have spiritually matured a great deal in three days, for the Scriptures tell us that even His parents were amazed that He was dialoging so wisely with the temple leaders.

It is not difficult to understand why Mary was upset and anxious after searching for her missing Son! In fact, it's easy to feel her anxiety. When they finally were able to question Jesus, His response was open and simple: "Why do you seek Me? Did you not know that I must be about My Father's business?" (Luke 2:49).

His parents "did not understand the statement which He spoke to them" (v. 50). Jesus' response was not disrespectful or rude, although it is often misunderstood that way. His parents did not completely understand the relationship that Jesus had to His Heavenly Father, nor could they have understood Jesus' ultimate destination of the Cross. It should have been clear to His parents that He would have waited in the temple. Where else would He be but in His Father's house?

Although we know that understanding of Jesus' ultimate purpose was not yet known by Mary, this instance was an important turning point for her. Seeing Jesus both learning and dialoging in the temple at such a tender age was such a powerful image that Luke 2:51 specifically mentioned that Mary "kept all these things in her heart." Years later this incident in the temple was so firmly fixed in Mary's memory that she shared the experience with Luke—who included it in his gospel.

Then He went down with them and came to Nazareth, and was subject to them, but His mother kept all these things in her heart. And Jesus increased in wisdom and stature, and in favor with God and men. (Luke 2:51–52)

As Mary watched Jesus pass through different stages in His life, she must have done a great deal of meditating in these years while seeking the Lord's guidance and direction. The Spirit kept teaching and guiding her, helping her to always remember the Lord and His ways. Perhaps the song God gave her during her pregnancy kept her heart steadfast on Him. Keeping all these things that the Lord had revealed to her in her heart would have a much deeper impact in the days to come.

THE SILENT YEARS

"And Jesus increased in wisdom and stature, and in favor with God and men" (Luke 2:52). This maturity was the result of the keen steward-ship of Mary and Joseph during Christ's early childhood. After Jesus was found in the temple, the Scripture indicates that Jesus "went down with them and came to Nazareth, and was subject [obedient] to them" (v. 51). Although Jesus could have chosen many different roads, He sought to honor His parents through His obedience to their guidance.

From this time until Jesus began His ministry at about thirty years of age, we hear nothing about His developmental or teenage years. Some call these the "silent years," which suggest that the Gospels focused only on the significant stages between boyhood and maturity.[11] However, the stewardship of Jesus' life by Mary continued to be real and obvious. Joseph, Mary's husband and Jesus' earthly father, had possibly died during this time.

When Jesus appears again, He is fully mature, confident of the Father's will, and ready to continue in His obedience. Mary will have been a major factor in all this, in spite of her questions about His life. She knew her stewardship and responsibility and was obediently faithful, as she had promised. Mary continued with her Son throughout His ministry and through the horrors of His cruel death. She remained through the Resurrection and Ascension and brought her strong faith into the life in the early church.

Stewardship of her Son, Jesus, brought unexpected choices, pain, and sorrow. She faced struggles to embrace the unfolding of God's activity around her and to her, yet she remembered God's revelation and continued to keep all things in her heart (Luke 2:19). God reaffirmed His work many times through others around her, bringing encouragement that Mary would need later in life. For Mary's faith was not based on something that she didn't know, but on what she did know and chose to believe (i.e., the Law— Luke 2:22–24, 41–42).

There are so many things we wish the Scripture told us, and so many questions we would like to ask. When the Scripture is silent or has not included something, there is a reason. We must, therefore, take a close look at what it does say and seek to understand the importance of why these verses were included. What did God want us to understand from these passages?

Such precious moments of Mary's daily faith in God have been given to us through these passages of Scripture: Mary's experience at Jesus' birth and knowing of God's watch-care and provision for her, God's affirmation of their obedience to the laws, watching Jesus mature in His wisdom and faith in God, seeing Jesus grow in stature to all who encountered His life, and seeing her accept the path that God had chosen for her Son.

God included simple moments in her life and revealed how ordinary she was. She expressed normal responses to Jesus' growing up and to her ordinary carrying out of her responsibilities as a wife and mother. She struggled with fear and anxiety and with what God's plan in the future would hold for her Son.

At the same time that we see Mary in the ordinary, the Scripture allows us to see the depth of Mary's character. She allowed God to adjust her life, her dreams, and her future and followed Him in obedience. There is no mention of anger or bitterness for what she struggled through, but only a continued daily trust in God to guide her.

Later, it was her other son James who clarified that "faith without works is dead" (James 2:20). Mary was also an influence over James. James saw the faith that led to obedience and involvement in God's work and wrote, "Faith was working together with his works, and by works faith was made perfect" (v. 22). Mary clearly modeled both faith and works, which then gave God the freedom to complete His work through her. What a wonderful testimony for Mary's life!

Correct understanding about the Scripture and its truths is essential, but it is empty without being expressed by the way we live our lives. Without our lives being lived out daily in obedience and faith, God cannot complete His work through us. Don't allow yourself to be satisfied with just having the right answers. Right answers cannot bring happiness or salvation. Growth comes only through trust and obedience to the Lord. There are many today who have a great deal of scriptural knowledge but do not practically apply it in their lives. God can't use a person who is not willing to live out His truths. Set your heart on obedience, like Mary did at an early age, and God will come and encounter your life in a special and unique way.

QUESTIONS FOR STUDY AND REFLECTION

1. We know that Jesus did not start out wise, but grew and became strong in the Spirit and filled with wisdom. Are you seeking to grow daily in Christ? Are you helping your own children or the children you work with to "become strong in the Spirit" as Mary did?

2. Mary's faith was based on her knowledge of the Lord through the Scriptures and all that He had revealed in her life. It was not blind trust, but trust in her God that had proven Himself faithful. Are you seeking and striving to grow in your knowledge of the Lord through the Scriptures? Are you always seeking to remember your God who has been faithful to you?

3. When Mary found Jesus at the temple, it was clear that God was working in and through His life. Although Mary may not have always understood, she always remembered what God was doing in her Son's life. Are you increasingly aware of God's activity in the lives of your children? What are you seeing, and how are you responding to God working in and through them? Are you writing it down for them so that later you can reveal all that God has shown you for their life?

4. Mary had to release Jesus and allow Him to obey His Father—no matter what the cost. Are you "holding on" to your children, or have you released them to God who gave them to you? Have you trusted the Lord with their future?

CHAPTER 10

THE YEARS OF JESUS' MINISTRY

The Spirit of the LORD is upon Me, because He has anointed Me to preach the gospel to the poor; He has sent Me to heal the broken-hearted, to proclaim liberty to the captives and recovery of sight to the blind, to set at liberty those who are oppressed; to proclaim the acceptable year of the LORD.
—LUKE 4:18–19; COMPARE ISA. 61:1–2

OBEDIENCE CONTINUES to be a prevalent theme as we look at the next stage in Mary's life with Jesus. In her first encounter with God and His will, she surrendered to Him with "let it be to me according to your word" (Luke 1:38). She faithfully lived out this commitment throughout the rest of her life. This was especially true during the ministry years of Jesus' life. Each revelation she experienced, she kept in her heart. She would recall her commitment to the Lord. The Holy Spirit enabled and brought understanding to Mary as she sought to obey. Quietly yet faithfully, God enabled her to respond to Jesus' ministry in letting God be God in and through her and her Son, Jesus.

God chose for the Scripture to pass through Jesus' adolescence in silence, as well as through what we would consider young adulthood, bringing us to the start of His earthly ministry at the age of thirty. As mentioned in the previous chapter, Jesus was in the process of breaking away from traditional expectations and family roles, yielding His life fully to what the Father had sent Him to do.

As Jesus begins His ministry, even less is said about His mother, Mary. The focus of the Gospels turns completely to what God is doing through His Son to redeem the world. There are eighteen years of silence, from when Jesus was twelve years old to when He began His ministry. We must be cautious when we reason from silence. However, it seems Mary continued to mature in her walk with God through much meditation. During these years, Zacharias and Elizabeth may have had many special conversations with her, perhaps teaching her from Scripture. The Gospels provide us with a brief look at Mary's continuing presence in the life of Jesus and the adjustments she had to make to allow God to continue working through her. They also clearly show how Mary had to make a choice in allowing Jesus to fulfill God's plans for His life—and not her plans or dreams for Him!

FAMILY SUPPORT

Having two children of my own, I (Carrie) now have a great deal of respect for my mother! Four boys and one girl would be more than a handful for any parent. My parents always tried to raise us with the understanding that our future belonged to the Lord we served. We shouldn't claim to love the Lord if we aren't ready to obey Him when He places a call on our lives. This principle continues to be very real in my life. When my husband and I prayed about our call to missions and subsequently our call to Germany, the only dilemma we faced was if this was truly of the Lord. I knew that God could lead me anywhere in the world, and my parents would support our decision. They raised me to know God's voice, and they trusted my relationship with God to know His will. More importantly, they trusted the God we serve to always be faithful and give us His best.

Sadly, I have encountered many missionaries who bear a heavy burden for having to choose God over their family. Often when these families and/or individuals return home from the mission field, instead of it being a joyous experience, it is painful and difficult. When I look at my own children, although they are still young, I always try to keep in mind that they belong to the Lord—and not me! Everything I teach them should prepare their lives to know and experience Him. As Mary had to release Jesus, so must each of us release our children to the Lord.

When I look at my own children, although they are still young, I always try to keep in mind that they belong to the Lord—and not me! . . . As Mary had to release Jesus, so must each of us release our children to the Lord.

JESUS' FAMILY

After seeing Jesus in the temple at the age of twelve and knowing that He was growing in wisdom and favor with God and man, we see Him beginning His ministry at the age of thirty (Luke 3:23). Thirty was an important age within the Jewish society, as it was the legal age of maturity.[1] It was also the year that the Levites were able to be considered to begin their priestly duties in the temple.[2] Knowing that there are no unimportant details to the Lord, it is no coincidence that Jesus began His ministry at this culturally important age.

Although His early years would have been heavily influenced by His mother's teaching, His later developmental years would have been spent learning the trade of the family—carpentry. We can assume that Jesus had been intricately involved in His family, taking care of His mother, and possibly running or at least learning to run the family carpentry business. Joseph quietly and steadily had a strong influence over Jesus' life as Jesus is clearly seen as "the carpenter" or "the carpenter's son."

Then He went out from there and came to His own country, and His disciples followed Him. And when the Sabbath had come, He began to teach in the synagogue. And many hearing Him were astonished, saying, "Where did this Man get these things? And what wisdom is this which is given to Him, that such mighty works are performed by His hands! Is this not the carpenter, the Son of Mary, and brother of James, Joses, Judas, and Simon? And are not His sisters here with us?" (Mark 6:1–3)

From Scripture and from the historical understanding we have of the culture, we know that a business or trade was a family concern. There are several examples in the New Testament of families working together in a trade. Within the Jewish culture, it was expected that the father would teach his son a craft or trade, and sometimes a whole town would concentrate on one craft or industry.[3] Jesus was seen as the son of a carpenter. Normally, the business and responsibilities for the family would rest with the father—or in case of his death, the oldest son. For others in the community to recognize Jesus through His trade also speaks well of His hard work and integrity. But it is this family business that Jesus, at the age of thirty, left behind to follow God's plan for His life. He understood what it would mean—not only for His disciples—but also for us, to leave family and security to follow God's will for our lives.

Trusting as God Leads

by Julie Cook

As a junior at Samford University, I had known for some time that God was leading me toward a ministry in music. I grew up in church and had been a Christian since the age of seven. I had been lovingly discipled over the years by several individuals and knew that God was crafting me for service for Him. Some of my friends wanted to be the next "great performer" in Christian music, yet I knew that was not to be my pursuit.

I had the opportunity to sing in the a cappella choir at Samford, which took frequent mission trips. On a mission trip to South Korea in 1985, I saw God at work in a very real and powerful way. Dr. Billy Kim, who had a daughter in our choir, was the pastor of the Korean church where we were able to see firsthand how God was using him to impact his country for Christ. I visited a large Christian church where many thousands gathered on Friday at midnight to pray. The excitement among the believers in Korea was infectious.

I was seeing a move of God that I would never forget. I prayed, "Lord, if You can use me, I'll be obedient. I won't list my limitations; I'll accept whatever assignment You give me. I want to make a difference for You. Please show me." I excitedly returned home, as I wanted to share with my home church my decision for Christian service. I don't think it was any surprise to my parents, my mentors, or my minister of music when I made my decision public. I wanted the affirmation of my home church, which they lovingly granted.

As I returned to school, I could not wait to share this with my New Testament professor—a man I highly regarded as a biblical scholar. I desperately needed his counsel. I made an appointment with Dr. Bryan to tell him how God was leading me, but I also wanted to tell him a very personal concern. I had not known many women in church ministry. I was told, "You'll have to go to a liberal church to be in leadership." How discouraging. I struggled with this. *How can it be that I know You've chosen me for salvation and are equipping me for ministry, and yet I'm being told by some that being a woman is a liability?* I knew in my heart that this did not match up. I did not want to pastor a church. I felt that one day I would marry and be a mother. But I clearly saw God's hand in my life gently leading me toward ministry.

The day of my appointment neared, and I was nervous. What would I be told? I placed great weight on what this beloved professor might say, but I went with a teachable spirit ready to hear what his thoughts were. I shared with him my heart and what God had shown me, and then I got to the heart of the matter.

"You see," I said hesitantly, "the only problem is—I'm a girl!" He smiled and listened attentively, waiting for me to take a breath, and said, "You just be obedient, although you don't see the whole picture. He will direct your steps."

Years later, God has done just that. When I was twenty-six, my home church hired me as the music associate directing the youth choir, assisting with the adult choir, and directing other ensembles. My mentor and minister of music spent much time investing in me, as he had been doing for a very long time. He gave me the opportunity to serve without regard to my gender. I know that God placed him in my life to pave the way for me in ministry. My church has been very supportive of me as a woman in music ministry leadership. Along the way, other women have come to encourage me and hold me accountable. And now God has begun to use me to encourage other women that He has placed around me.

I know that I must remain teachable in whatever role God has for me in the future. I pray that I will say, "Yes, Lord . . . may it be to me as You wish" when He gives me a new assignment. Obedience is costly. I wish there was a way around it, but there is not. Sometimes growth comes through suffering. I have dealt with a particular situation that I have cried and prayed for God to change, yet He chose to change me instead. Only then did I fully understand the sovereignty of God. I know now that nothing touches me except what is first sifted through His loving hands. He sees the whole tapestry of my life. I only see what is right before me. Either I trust Him, or I don't.

Rarely does He send me an outline of His will for me to approve, although I will admit I have asked at times! God sent me a loving husband, John, who is fully supportive of my role in the music ministry at our church, two wonderful children who depend on me to be what I say I am, and many people to sharpen and encourage me. I have learned over these many years to trust the fact that God will never lead me where His grace, guidance, and love can't keep me.

Julie's friendship has truly been a special gift from God at a time when I (Carrie) needed encouragement. Her genuine heart and willingness to serve the Lord in all things is an example to all of what God can do in a life that is committed to obedience.

THE CARPENTER'S SON

Mary watched closely as Jesus labored with Joseph. As the firstborn son, Jesus took the traditional role of the eldest son in taking responsibility over the family and ultimately for her. She watched as Jesus grew in favor with God, seeing Him grow in His habit in prayer and seeking wisdom from the Scriptures.

We are told in Mark 6:3 that Jesus was a "carpenter, the Son of Mary, and brother of James, Joses, Judas, and Simon," and that same verse tells us He also had sisters. Again in Matthew 13:55, "Is this not the carpenter's son?" Mary watched as Jesus' brothers and sisters grew up with Him and worked alongside Him daily. They would have seen Jesus' integrity, obedience, wisdom, faithfulness, and love of others, and they observed Him giving honor to their parents. They saw Jesus live out His everyday life before their eyes, but the Scripture says, "Even His brothers did not believe in Him" (John 7:5). Jesus, however, must have seen potential in James (His brother), as Jesus took extra time with him before His ascension for a special confirmation of His Messiahship (1 Cor. 15:7).

We do not know the reason for Jesus' brothers' unbelief in Him and all that He was doing around them. Being raised in the same household, it is surprising that Jesus' own family did not understand who He was. Yet sometimes it is the ones closest to us that have been blinded to who we are. Jesus Himself mentioned that "a prophet is not without honor except in his own country, among his own relatives, and in his own house" (Mark 6:4). It wasn't until after Jesus' death and resurrection that His brothers were counted among those who believed and were continuing in prayer in the upper room (Acts 1:14).

THE UNBELIEF OF OTHERS

Some did not believe in Jesus, even after His teaching and miracles. Every sincere servant of God will experience occasions when those who do not believe in Jesus will attempt to discourage or mock the believer. I (Henry) have experienced this during my ministry, and have struggled through some very difficult situations with those with whom we have worked. Some did not expect any hardship, so when the hard times came, they left us and the work completely. Others left us because we had to "walk by faith" for our salaries and financial support, and they said, "We cannot put our family in jeopardy this way." Some left us wanting to establish their own ministries. Some even listened to false reports and rumors about us and withdrew all financial support, thus putting us into great hardship. Some were jealous, like the Pharisees were of Jesus, and opposed us greatly also, seeking to destroy our ministry. God, however, stood with us and sustained us at all times.

We learned that when people opposed us in the completing of God's work, they were actually opposing our Lord who gave us the assignment. When we were faithful to do all that God had instructed, He openly blessed His work and brought the increase.

There will continue to be opposition within the ministry. A year does not go by in which we do not see another example of this type of opposition. Mary watched Jesus experience this deeply throughout His life—and in His death. He modeled how we can stand in the face of adversity and remain faithful. Our responsibility, therefore, is to always stay before the Lord, listen to His voice, and obey all His commands— regardless of the thoughts and actions of men.

THE BEGINNING OF JESUS' MINISTRY

As Jesus began His ministry, Mary and her family, along with Jesus and His disciples, were found at a wedding in Cana. Cana was a small, unimportant town that always had to be qualified with "in Galilee" to identify its location.[4] Jesus and His disciples were invited to attend a wedding celebration. It is unclear if this was a relative or close friend of the family, but it is clear that Mary was either in charge or helping with the feast preparations (John 2:3). This was no small task! A wedding during this time period was a huge event that could last for up to a week.[5]

This was most likely a poor family with humble origins that came upon a huge problem. In those days the people either drank water or wine, or watered-down wine! While they were making preparations for this event, they miscalculated how much wine they would need, and they were running out. This would have been a colossal embarrassment for this new couple! Mary understood the significance of this crisis and brought the problem to Jesus.

Mary knew her Son. She had watched throughout His life as He grew in wisdom and as He carried the responsibility for the family. She knew that Jesus could make the difference, addressing any problem or situation. So it was Jesus, her eldest child, to whom she turned in times of trouble.

When Mary came to Jesus, clearly expecting Him to resolve this problem, Jesus' remark could sound a bit harsh to our ears: "Woman, what does your concern have to do with Me? My hour has not yet come" (John 2:4). This statement expresses a turning point in Jesus' life. It is suggested that, although Jesus was speaking courteously for that cultural time-period, He was beginning to put a distance between Himself and His mother. When He was under His mother's care, He was also under her authority. Now, however, He was beginning His ministry years and did not need any outside influences (including from His mother) in His quest to follow God.[6]

Mary simply told the servants, "Whatever He says to you, do it" (John 2:5). There is no sign that Mary feels slighted by Jesus' answer. Mary knew her Son to be the Messiah. She knew her calling and especially remembered all the circumstances around His birth. She must have wondered when Jesus would fulfill God's plan for Him and when others would know the truth of who He was. There is complete trust and perhaps some motherly pride as she leaves things in His hands.

Jesus, using six stone pots filled with water, turned ordinary water into the finest wine. The Scripture says, "This beginning of signs [miracles]

Jesus did in Cana of Galilee, and manifested His glory; and His disciples believed in Him" (John 2:11). Unknowingly, Mary may have created the opportunity for Jesus to do His first miracle as He began His ministry. It is clear that the Father gave permission for Jesus to begin to manifest His glory, and His disciples believed in Him. Jesus was making a transition into full-time ministry in obedience to His Heavenly Father's will.

After the wedding, Mary, Jesus, His brothers, and Jesus' disciples all left and went down to Capernaum (John 2:12). Later, Mary and Jesus' brothers stood outside the crowds who were listening to Jesus teach and requested to see Him, calling Him away from His teaching and preaching. Here Jesus makes it clear that He is now fully following His Heavenly Father's agenda and not that of His mother or family. There is no indication as to what they wanted or how they responded to Him.

Jesus responded before the multitudes to His mother's request to see Him: For whoever does the will of God is My brother and My sister and mother" (Mark 3:35). This was not a rebuke or a rejection of His mother, and once again, there is no indication that she was offended by Him. It was clearly a public affirmation of the nature of the kingdom of God that awaits all who will believe and obey. The King had come—His kingdom of heaven was now near, and any and all who would believe and obey the Father could enter into a relationship with Him. His whole life was now immersed in teaching, preaching, and healing people to demonstrate this fact, and He instructed His disciples to do the same (Matt. 9:35; 10:7–8). It seems that now Mary fully releases Jesus to the Heavenly Father and His will for Jesus' life.

MINISTRY STEPS

Like Mary's life, my (Henry) entire ministry has been a progressive revelation and experience with God. Being faithful in a little, I found that

God continually gave me more. And each time I trusted and obeyed Him, He gave me new and fresh experiences and a deeper understanding in my relationship with Him.

When I first began serving the Lord in ministry, I began by teaching youth. I was then led to serve as a minister of music. This led to being asked to become the minister of music and education. After learning many things from each of these positions, the Lord led me to become the pastor. After several years, I was asked to be the pastoral missionary and church starter as well as the minister to students. This eventually led to being president of a theological college. Then God led me to become the director of missions over many churches in an association. Next, I served in denominational work, directing the office of Prayer, Revival & Spiritual Awakening at our Home Mission Board (now North American Mission Board). I also was asked to keep offices in the International Mission Board as well as the Sunday School Board. In retirement this has continued as I now work with top CEOs from major companies, the U.N., and the military, and am continually asked to speak to key groups nationally and internationally in more than one hundred countries.

These are progressive steps in my life and ministry. Did God call me to just one task or a specific career? No. He called me to a relationship with Himself. That means that as I follow Him, He can change my call and direction at any time—because He knows that I will obey Him, as He accomplishes His purposes through me.

Placing My Future in God's Hands
by Jan Carter

I knew God's calling on my life through an encounter with Him my sophomore year in college. I was pursuing my lifetime dream of becoming a veterinarian, when God drastically changed my focus to a career in nursing. I have been nursing now for twenty-three years and know without a doubt that this was God's calling on my life. I have spent twenty of the twenty-three years of my career in bedside nursing. At a time in my life when most of my peers' careers were settling down, mine made a drastic change.

I had been working part-time for about a year at a hospital and had begun filling in for company nurses at a large corporation. I was approached by my supervisor and manager about a full-time job. The company had committed to launching a comprehensive wellness program and needed someone to coordinate the many components of the program. After talking with my management, I realized this job would entail many aspects in which I had little or no experience. I asked for time to process this and see if I was interested.

I once again found myself confused and struggling with what God wanted me to do. I spent a week talking to God and my husband about it. I prayed extensively and had lengthy discussions with God. I knew it would be a great job, but I saw so much uncertainty and change with it. I had many reasons why I couldn't do the job—my lack of corporate experience, lack of needed computer skills, inexperience with occupational nursing, and many, many others. I knew the last thing God had told me to do was to work part-time and be available to my children. Was He telling me something different now? I wanted to be available to my family, including my parents, as they lived out of town and had both experienced major health problems. I needed to remain flexible with my work hours. I certainly didn't want to work five days a week in an office downtown in a large metropolitan city.

I wrestled with God through tears, but I had determined in my heart that I would seek Him only for my answer. I talked with my husband, but he knew I had to hear a word from God, and he offered only support and not advice. After one week of seeking God's direction, He clearly gave me His word on the matter. I had emptied myself to the point of "whatever it takes." I wanted to be obedient and knew that only through obedience would I find peace and happiness.

God took me to the Word using my Oswald Chambers devotional. The title for the day was "Don't think now, just take the road." The text was Matthew 14 where Peter walked on the water to Jesus. Peter could only see the billowing waves, not Jesus and what He had for him. I, too, was only seeing the waves and why I couldn't do this job. I certainly didn't want to take a job and then fail. God then took me to the words of a friend who was going through a very difficult time in his life. He told me that he focused on the words of a spiritual leader and friend, "Everything that comes to the believer's life has been filtered by God," and we must look for God's activity around us. Was this God's activity? I didn't want to work full-time, but could God be telling me that He had something different for me now?

My final spiritual marker came that same morning during my continued prayers. He clearly spoke to me to say, "I call missionaries to the jungles of Africa and Venezuela, and I'm only calling you to the state of Georgia." He also reminded me that foreign missionaries take their immediate family members with them, but their extended family members and friends make sacrifices. I was broken at this word. I immediately wept and asked God's forgiveness for whining and objecting about the challenges and what it would cost me. His call on my life at this moment was clear. I again had encountered God, and what would I do with this encounter? I knew the concept that "if He calls you to it, He will equip you," but now I would have to live it.

I told my husband and children of my decision, and they were excited and very supportive. My sixteen-year-old immediately thought of ways she could help with her younger sibling and told me that if

God was telling me to do it, I didn't have any other choice. Once I gave in to God's calling, even amidst the fear and uncertainty, I felt peace and excitement to know I was right in the center of God's will. I was eager to watch Him work. It has been a wonderful journey, not an easy one, but it has been exciting to see God use the inadequacies of one so ordinary to achieve great things that are touching the lives of many. Many of my objections and concerns have been answered by God to allow me flexibility and availability to my family. I truly believe this wellness program is God's blessing on a company that is full of godly believers who choose to honor Him in their workplace through their integrity and commitment to serving others. I'm so thrilled to be a part of it. At a point in my life when I might think that my career would be winding down to a comfortable and slower pace, God is taking me on perhaps my most exciting journey yet.

We have both known Jan for several years and have watched her accept each challenge from the Lord with a sweet and joyful heart. Her peace in the Lord is visible, and her walk with Him is deep and unwavering. It was exciting for me (Carrie) to be a part of her Sunday school class at our home church and see her excitement that comes from learning more about the Lord. We look forward to seeing how God is going to continue to work in and through her life in the years to come.

Mary's life was a progressive revelation from God, trusting Him to fulfill all His promises to her. She needed His wisdom to help her complete His purposes for her life, and she remained obedient through every step.

Since her call from the Lord, Mary's life had been extraordinary. She was seeing her Son do amazing and wonderful things. She watched Him continue to grow in wisdom and knowledge of the Lord, and she must have been humbled to know that God had indeed granted her favor. And yet, right after these exciting days of Jesus' ministry comes His death on the cross. God had been continually preparing Mary, giving a greater and deeper understanding of Jesus and her relationship to Him. Jesus' relationship to her was about to move from "eldest son" to Savior!

Looking at Mary's responses and involvement with Jesus during His three and a half years of ministry, it is essential to think from God's perspective. Here is truly where Mary "decreases," and Jesus and the Father's will "increase." We saw this in John the Baptist's life in the course of this same time period. John openly acknowledged that "I baptize with water, but there stands One among you whom you do not know. It is He who, coming after me, is preferred before me, whose sandal strap I am not worthy to loose . . . He must increase, but I must decrease" (John 1:26–27; 3:30). Although John had a powerful ministry, he had to "decrease" so that Jesus could "increase" and complete His Father's assignment.

During Jesus' ministry the people were now in the full presence of God, who was moving in the midst of His people to reveal His love and His purposes and redeem a lost world. God does not hide His purposes but expresses them so clearly that anyone seeking Him by faith will find Him! Jesus now points everyone to the Father in all He teaches and preaches and does.

Mary had to let Jesus go from His obligation to her as the oldest son. Probably a widow, since Joseph is not mentioned again, she could have demanded more of Jesus' time and watch-care over her. Instead, her trust was on the promises of God and His revealed will to her.

Scripture does not reveal any more about Mary's spiritual growth during these years, but she clearly remained faithful to her God whom she loved. Whenever Mary touched Jesus' life during these ministry years, Jesus continually turned her to the Father's will now being expressed through Him. He was also helping to prepare her, giving her the assurance that He was following the will of the Father. For Jesus did love His mother and, knowing that in the coming days He would face His own death, He sought to prepare her for what that would mean. Ultimately, who was Mary's family? Who was her son? "Whoever does the will of God is My brother and My sister and mother" (Mark 3:35).

For Mary, the new church was about to become a family who would care and provide for her, and John, who had a deep love for Jesus, was about to become her "son."

QUESTIONS FOR STUDY AND RESPONSE

1. We see Jesus at the beginning of His ministry leaving family, His work/business, and personal security and comforts to follow God's will for His life. Are you willing to give up everything and follow God's plan for your life? Are you obediently doing this?

2. The Scripture records the names of several of Jesus' brothers who were also with Mary, yet they did not believe in Jesus. Do you have unbelieving children or family members? Continue in your obedience to God, knowing that they will be watching to see the difference only He can make. He may use your life and your obedience to draw them to Himself.

3. Mary had to "decrease" in Jesus' life in order for Him to follow God in obedience. Are you willing to "decrease" in your children's lives, giving them the freedom to seek after their Lord?

4. Mary deeply loved her Son, yet there were times that she didn't understand His ways. Jesus' family probably loved Him and held a great deal of respect for their oldest brother, but they didn't believe Him to be the Messiah. It wasn't until later that they understood Him to be the Savior and believed in His name. Their hearts were changed as they saw the truth revealed in Christ. Have you recognized a time when you misunderstood God's ways or had a false understanding of a person's character? Did you allow God to work in your heart to reveal the truth to you? Have you always sought to

have a teachable spirit, or can you admit a mistake? Ask the Lord to always help you see the truth about Jesus and His ways. Ask Him to help you see the truth in people around you so that you don't miss what God wants to do through them to teach you! Be teachable, admit mistakes, and learn from Him!

5. Has God come to you recently and revealed His plan for your life? If not, search your heart to make sure that it is fully committed to obey His every command, and then live with confident expectation. Where God has you now is not an end in itself, but a stage from which to lead you into a deeper relationship with Him.

CHAPTER 11

MARY'S EXPERIENCE AFTER THE RESURRECTION

Now there stood by the cross of Jesus His mother, and His mother's sister, Mary the wife of Clopas, and Mary Magdalene. When Jesus therefore saw His mother, and the disciple whom He loved standing by, He said to His mother, "Woman, behold your son!" Then He said to the disciple, "Behold your mother!" And from that hour that disciple took her to his own home.

—JOHN 19:25–27

MARY'S LIFE CONTINUES to be mentioned in the Scriptures throughout the death of her Son and in the beginnings of the early Church. Again, there are many questions for which we would like answers. However, the Bible is not focusing on any one person—only on what God had done and was about to do through a people who would believe in Him. The passages that include Mary are very significant, because they show us glimpses into her life, enabling us to see how God continued to be faithful in expressing His love toward her. Though there are silent years in Mary's life and in Jesus' life, it is obvious God was with her just as He promised.

As we noted earlier, Mary was apparently now a widow. No mention in the Scripture is made regarding the death of Joseph, but it is thought he died before Jesus' ministry began. She had several other children who were referenced, revealing an aspect of Mary's family besides Jesus. From a cultural perspective of that time period, Mary's plight would look grim. She had lost her husband and chose to remain a widow. Then her oldest Son, who tradition dictates would care and provide for her, was brutally killed.

This would seem to be a lonely and desperate situation for anyone. Yet when the Scriptures mention Mary, she is never alone. God provided companions who would walk with her throughout her days. These were not just any companions! They were companions who had known and believed in her Son, who could understand her pain and help her heart heal and stay pure before the Lord. Life would be hard, although not uncertain, because of God's promises to her. When God's purposes were complete through Jesus, He did not then leave her on her own! He continued to love and care for her, providing not only for her spiritual needs but for her emotional and physical needs as well.

GOD'S PROVISION FOR MARY

Mary was a widow; this alone would have given her "special status" before the Lord. God expressed His compassion for widows all through the Bible (Deut. 10:18–19; Pss. 10:18; 146:9), and He emphasized how important it was to care for them. James summarized God's concern for the widows by writing, "Pure and undefiled religion before God and the Father is this: to visit orphans and widows in their trouble" (James 1:27).

God would not have expressed His heart for widows only to neglect Mary, the human mother of His Son, Jesus. So in Mary's widowhood, we see many other women walking with her. The Gospels record many instances of the women who were with Jesus (see Matt. 27:55–56; Mark 15:40–41; Luke 23:49, 55–56; 24:1–10). Some are clearly spoken of as His friends, believers, followers, and some are women that Jesus had healed. It is these women that John 19:25 mentions as being with Mary at the time of Jesus' death: "Now there stood by the cross of Jesus His mother, and His mother's sister, Mary the wife of Clopas, and Mary Magdalene."

No mention is made of the other disciples, besides John, or of Jesus' other siblings standing at the cross with Mary. Again, Jesus never did or said anything accidentally or even casually, but intentionally. But God faithfully provided companions for Mary to help her in her pain and loneliness, and she did not have to live out these days alone.

LONESOME PATHS

Although I (Carrie) am close to my family, I have spent almost half of my life living a great distance from them. Today, I have three brothers living in Canada, my parents live in the United States, and another brother lives in Norway. With Wendell and I living in Germany, it is very difficult to coordinate a family reunion! Often, following God's call for my life has led to some lonely places. Whether you are in church work, business, or another calling that takes you away from your family, it can lead to some very lonesome paths.

While I was in the midst of one lonely experience, I was feeling sorry for myself and thought I'd make sure God understood how I felt. Little did I know that God had been waiting for me to turn to Him in my loneliness. He had already made provisions for me, but since I was concentrating so hard on my situation, I literally missed what God had planned. Because the friendship didn't look like what I thought I needed, I almost missed it! Instead of a nice American friend that I could relate to, God gave me a special friendship with a local German that I could learn from. God chose to bless me, not with the friendship I thought I wanted, but with the friendship that I needed—quite a difference! What a shock it was when God revealed the friendship He had for me, which continues to this day. I learned to never focus on my circumstance or situation but to trust the Lord to provide me with all my needs. I continue to experience God this way, and He has faithfully provided companions with like-minded hearts.

THE PROVISION OF JOHN

Even in the very moment when Jesus was carrying the load of the world's sin and providing salvation for all mankind, He never forgot His responsibility as the eldest son. This responsibility was to care for His mother and give her security in her older years. From the cross, He felt the impending loneliness His mother would face after His death. There would undoubtedly be years that Mary would remember His life and His untimely and horrible death at the hands of cruel men. She would need a tender and thoughtful person to care for her. Jesus loved John and knew his heart, not only for Him, but possibly for His mother also.

Of all His disciples, John seemed to have a special place in the heart of Jesus. After guiding and instructing John for three and a half years, Jesus knew him thoroughly and intimately. So real was His trust in John that He would commit to him the keeping of His mother. John is called "the disciple whom Jesus loved" (see John 13:23; 20:2; 19:26, 21:7). It should be noted all these references to John as "the disciple whom Jesus loved" are found in John's gospel. He knew this was a special relationship and humbly bore witness to this. He was purposefully loved by Jesus, for Jesus knew the assignment He would give John to care for His mother.

As Mary was watching her Son on the cross, she heard Him commend her to "the beloved disciple" regarding her watch-care. This passage is recorded in John's gospel:

When Jesus therefore saw His mother, and the disciple whom He loved standing by, He said to His mother, "Woman, behold your son!" Then He said to the disciple, "Behold your mother!" And from that hour that disciple took her to his own home. (John 19:26–27)

Notice that Jesus did not entrust Mary to His own brothers or sisters. There is no evidence that they knew Him as John did, nor is there clear evidence that they were, at this point, trusted followers of His.

From these Scriptures, we have a glimpse of the last years of Mary's life. Mary's last days were spent with John, the beloved disciple of Jesus, whom Jesus entrusted with His mother's life from that point on.

GODLY COMPANIONSHIP

I (Henry) have noticed with great joy that God has not left me alone or in any way isolated. I have been granted some of the finest companions who have come alongside my life as I have tried faithfully to live out God's call to me.

In our first church God sent Larry Thomas to be an associate with me, along with his wife, Gail. In Saskatoon God gave us companions to match each aspect of our ministry. In church planting God gave us Len Koster and Jack Conner; in student work God sent Robert Cannon; in our theological college God added Barbra Burkett; and in our work in revival and awakening, God gave us Ron and Patricia Owens. Now, in our new ministry, He has given us Clayton and Lois Quattlebaum and many wonderful volunteers. Like Mary, every called servant of God will be given vital companions so that he or she can finish well.

THE RESURRECTION AND ASCENSION

Mary now had the assuring presence of companions at the time of Jesus' death and did not have to experience all these other times alone. She was not mourning for her Son alone, but while God was preparing to complete His purposes with the Resurrection, He provided the comfort Mary needed.

Then came the resurrection of Jesus. What a moment for Mary! She is not singled out during the resurrection days but is mentioned as being with other women (John 19:25 and later in the Upper Room in Acts 1:14). We could assume that she was with the other women caring for the body of Jesus. "They, and certain other women with them, came to the tomb bringing the spices which they had prepared" (Luke 24:1).

Mary, in the midst of the women and the disciples, sought to work through the reality of Jesus' resurrection, remembering that Jesus had said He would be raised to life again in three days (Mark 8:31). What a personal joy it must have been to not only see her Son but her Savior!

Jesus was with them forty days teaching and guiding them, and then directing them to wait in Jerusalem "until you are endued with Power from on high" (Luke 24:49). The Holy Spirit was about to come, and Mary was one who listened to Jesus and was obedient by waiting with the believers. What a statement that would have made to the other followers of Jesus.

Mary's presence was important to the early Church. Every believer is important to the others. The writer of Hebrews urged every believer "not forsaking the assembling of ourselves together . . . but exhorting one another . . ." (Heb. 10:25).

MARY IN THE UPPER ROOM

Mary's presence is purposefully recorded as being a vital part of the early church family, especially those 120 who gathered in an upper room in Jerusalem, as Jesus had commanded them to do.

When they [the 11 disciples] had entered [Jerusalem], they went up into the upper room where they were staying . . . These all continued with one accord in prayer and supplication, with the women and Mary the mother of Jesus, and with His brothers. (Acts 1:13–14)

This special naming of Mary is of great importance. Her presence and her quiet and godly influence were crucial—especially for the women. Mary seems to be a catalyst for the affirmation of women in the early believers. There is a constant reference to women who followed and supported Jesus, and He affirmed them. Women had a significant place in the purposes of God.

This mention of the 120 is followed by the powerful record in Acts 2 of Pentecost and the coming and filling of each with the Holy Spirit. It clearly says, "They were all filled with the Holy Spirit" (v. 4). This moment would have included Mary! Mary experienced the complete understanding of what God did through her Son. She had known that Jesus was the Messiah, but now she was encountering Him as her living Lord! What peace that must have brought to her, knowing that her Son's pain and suffering fulfilled God's purposes of salvation.

Peter would then preach his mighty sermon, which led to the beginning of the Church. He would speak of the life of Christ and announce to all that this phenomenon was in fulfillment of the prophecy of Joel. "And also on My menservants and on My maidservants I will pour out My Spirit in those days" (Joel 2:29, quoted by Peter in Acts 2:18).

We don't hear any more specifically of Mary, or her life in the early Church in Jerusalem, or later with John in Ephesus. God knew that to exalt Mary (the vessel) over Jesus would be the tendency of the human heart. So no more mention is made of her, only that she was a real and vital member in the early Church in Jerusalem during the days following the ascension of Jesus.

MARY'S INTERDEPENDENCE

Mary, like all other believers, was not to be "alone" as she fulfilled God's will in her life. At the beginning of her following of God's revealed will for her life, she received the good and godly counsel of older and mature people of God, who themselves had been faithfully doing God's will for their lives. God designed from the beginning of creation for His children to be interdependent.

Her cousin Elizabeth encouraged her greatly, and for three months Zacharias also must have taught her from Scriptures. Simeon and Anna, in the temple, were important people in her early life of obedience. They were thoroughly versed in the Old Testament Scriptures and were able to give much needed counsel and encouragement. All through Jesus' growing years, Mary would have received godly counsel and encouragement.

In our day, older, mature adults must be walking with every believer to guide and teach strategically. God made us interdependent too! Each of us must have someone to consult with who can encourage us in doing what we know clearly to be God's will in our life. Mature believers must be available to other believers. This is God's purpose for us.

Mary remained within the fellowship of God's people, who were a great encouragement to her. Being a part of God's fellowship of believers should also be greatly encouraging for each of us. It is within the believing community, the Church, that God's planned interdependence for every believer in knowing and doing the will of God is made clear. And remember, His Great Commission assignment for us is accompanied by the same Holy Spirit and the "power of the Highest" to overshadow us. "And lo, I am with you always, even to the end of the age" (Matt. 28:20).

When the "I am" is with us, "the power of the Highest will overshadow" us (Luke 1:35), giving us all we need to accomplish His assignment.

Paul prayed for all God's people to have "the eyes of your understanding . . . enlightened; that you may know . . . what is the exceeding greatness of His power toward us who believe" (Eph. 1:18–19). Mary was given God's perspective, and God can give it to us, too!

The Presence of God

by Jan Johnsonius

It happened in a split second. And forever my world was changed. A cold, damp winter night in the pampas of Argentina. A two-lane road practically in the middle of nowhere. A sudden swerving of the vehicle, and then flipping over, and over, and over again. One life ended, and another severely damaged and devastated, and yet . . .

We had been serving as missionaries in Argentina for just under a year when my husband, Jim, and I were involved in a terrible auto accident. An accident that claimed Jim's life and left me struggling to live—not just physically, but emotionally and spiritually as well. That night I was changed forever. Not so much for what I lost—my husband, my best friend, my partner in ministry, my home, my place of service, my health—but for what I gained.

Does that sound strange? Yes, I suppose it would. Even now I cannot fully explain it. I guess that is an inextricable part of an encounter with the living God—it is often difficult to put into human words. But that night, as I was writhing in pain and struggling between life and death, and already beginning to mourn the loss of Jim, I cannot describe it any other way than the amazing, encompassing, holy, and all-loving presence of God. I experienced a peace that passes all understanding. And I recognized, really recognized for the first time, the depth of God's love for me. I had never truly seen it before— perhaps because without knowing it I was leaning on the things of this world—my husband, my health, a place to live, a ministry. But in a split second all that was stripped away. I was left naked and bleeding, without family, without a home—literally.

And in that moment all that remained was me and God. Nothing else. Nothing to come between. Only His peace. His presence. And suddenly I realized I had all that I would ever need. That His love was sufficient. That He was my all in all. And I knew that I was forever changed. Not because of the accident but because of my encounter with God. And that what I had gained that evening could never be taken from me. My life. The life God had always wanted me to have— to know Him as He desired me to know Him.

Now, I would never say that everything was beautifully perfect after that. Obviously not! The heartache and the pain, both physical and emotional, were practically unbearable. There were times when I truly would have rather died in that accident and been present with the Lord. And yet, in every moment, Christ was with me. Carrying me, comforting me, sustaining me, showing me Himself. His presence was nearly palpable. And His love . . . how can I begin to describe it?

As the years have passed, He has continued to be faithful, to be my Husband and my Father, as His Word clearly says He will be. I have learned to live fully in His words that say "My grace is sufficient for you, for my power is made perfect in weakness," and to echo Paul's reply, "Therefore I will boast all the more gladly about my weaknesses, so that Christ's power may rest on me. That is why, for Christ's sake, I delight in weaknesses, in insults, in hardships, in persecutions, in difficulties. For when I am weak, then I am strong" (2 Cor. 12:9–10 NIV).

I learned to identify with Job, not so much for what He lost, as for what he gained. For in those moments when everything is stripped away from us, and we are left with all that truly matters—the presence of Christ—we can each say from the depths of our souls, "I have heard of You by the hearing of the ear, but now my eye sees You" (Job 42:5). Blessed be the Name.

I (Carrie) first met Jan in seminary while we were both working on our Master of Divinity degrees in Texas. Almost immediately we were the best of friends. I have watched Jan grow and change through the years as God brought her closer to Himself. She has always had a deeply personal and fervent relationship with the Lord and has sought to follow His will for her life. Our friendship has only grown stronger as we are now colleagues on the mission field in Western Europe.

Jan completed her degree and was appointed as a career missionary to Madrid, Spain. There, she works as the team leader for the college and student ministry and has seen God do some mighty works. I continue to be thankful that God connected our lives, both through our friendship and our ministry together, and look forward to seeing all that God will do in the future.

NOT TO BE ALONE

When I (Henry) was seventeen years old, my life experienced God's clear claim and call into a lifetime of serving Him in the ministry. While I was attending seminary at the age of twenty-six, my dad, whom I deeply loved, died. This was very painful for me, and I have had to live my remaining days without him and his wise and godly counsel. A very few years later, my mother also died of cancer. I was then without parents to counsel and encourage me in some of my formative years of ministry. God placed others in my life, as He did for Mary. I deeply missed my parents, but God gave me a godly, happy, and wonderful wife with whom I have shared my ministry. God is so good!

MARY'S CLOSING YEARS

Because the Scripture does not clearly talk about Mary's latter years, we look to what we know about her previous obedience and to tradition for any other information about her life. Scripture tells us that she obeyed the last statement her Son made to her and went immediately with John. This would tell us that John took Mary with him as a part of his family. One of the traditions indicates that John took her to his home in Jerusalem, where she stayed for a number of years. There is a church in her honor in Jerusalem to this day. But the most likely tradition indicates that Mary went with John to Ephesus. It was here that John would later pastor and care for Mary until her death. Here also, there is a Church of Mary in Ephesus and a traditional site for her burial.

It is said that she lived a quiet and godly life, remembering her Son Jesus, His life and His death and His resurrection, and encouraging all of the believers around her. She remembered intensely her initial encounter with God's will through Gabriel and God's faithfulness to her from her teen years to her older age.

Even as Jesus was dying on the cross, He provided care and security for Mary, His mother. The infinite love of the Son of God! Mary's oldest, and her very special gift of God, knew and loved her deeply. And it would appear that for three and a half years of His ministry, Jesus expressed a deep and special love to John. He did not choose one of His earthly brothers, or even one of the other disciples. He chose John. Jesus knew what his response would be. He may have even spoken with him about this special charge that he would be given. Jesus' assignment of His mother to John seems to have been readily and immediately accepted. Again, we hear His carefully recorded words from the cross: "When Jesus therefore saw His mother, and the disciple whom He loved standing by . . . He said to the disciple 'Behold your mother!' And from that hour that disciple took her to his own home" (John 19:26–27).

GOD'S POWER

Having served as a pastor for thirty years, I (Henry) have walked with many through tough and often tragic times. I have such a deep commitment to the presence and power of the risen and living Savior that I always point them to Him. In thirty-plus years of pastoring (in California and Canada) I only saw one couple divorce. The husband had moved out of the country, and we were unable to present the power of God's Word to him for the healing of his marriage. I have seen our risen Lord heal families and lives and churches in countless numbers, as a witness to His Presence with His people today.

I have also seen this same Presence guide all five of our children into great marriages, into college and seminary, and into ministry with their Lord. They, too, have a deep love for God and for His people—and especially for knowing and doing the will of God.

We have been through very tough times—to this very day—but the "favor of God" continues to rest on us as we experience Him and His grace.

Mary's life could have come to a spiritual standstill because of the devastation she experienced at the Cross. She could have rejected the Father and all that He had shown her, because at that moment in time, she couldn't see His bigger picture. Yet she chose to keep her trust and faith in the Lord. She chose to listen to Jesus' dying words regarding John, allowing him to be her caregiver, instead of returning to a family that didn't believe in Jesus. She chose to surround herself with Jesus' friends and companions, allowing them to console and care for her. She remained in prayer, faithfully following Jesus' words to remain until they received power—and then God opened her eyes, and His salvation was revealed! But oh, she could have missed everything by not continuing in obedience. Yet Mary finished out her life always following her Lord, loving Him through all her days.

It is essential to recognize the importance of the companions that became such an integral part of Mary's life. If we don't, their purpose and role in God's bigger picture can be lost. Quietly, but surely, they became an influence over Mary's life. We have mentioned extensively the timely presence of Zacharias and Elizabeth. Mary realized early that she needed to be interdependent with other believers. She was not to live out her life as a loner, or in isolation, even though she knew she was "favored of God."

When Jesus' ministry began, women (especially those like Mary Magdalene whose life was radically saved by Jesus) began to follow Jesus. This was out of great respect, admiration, and love. Mary was soon involved with them, as together they followed Jesus. This became particularly noticeable as Jesus moved toward the Cross. Mary would need the friendship of other women who were following and supporting Jesus and His disciples. During the dark night of the soul Mary faced in the death of her Son, these other women were her sustaining companions. They remained together through the burial and then the resurrection of Jesus, and were even together in the Upper Room praying and fellowshipping before Pentecost. They also remained together in the early Church in Jerusalem.

The young apostle John, who was much loved by Jesus and who himself loved Jesus, became a special companion to Mary until the end of her days. But Mary's involvement in the life of the Church in Jerusalem was also significant in the long-term support she would need immediately following the events of the death, resurrection, and ascension of Jesus.

In the mind of God, parents are special, and we are to give them special care. Exodus 20:12 commands, "Honor your father and your mother." Jesus honored His mother, even from the cross. We must take seriously this command of God for our parents also.

Also, widows are special and precious to the heart of God. James 1:27 instructs us: "Pure and undefiled religion before God and the Father is this: to visit orphans and widows in their trouble, and to keep oneself unspotted from the world." Do not be surprised or resistant or even disappointed if God allows a friend, rather than family, to care for you in your latter years. Jesus chose to entrust His mother to His closest follower instead of other brothers or family members. God's ways are not our ways!

Do not be surprised or resistant or even disappointed if God allows a friend, rather than family, to care for you in your latter years. Jesus chose to entrust His mother to His closest follower instead of other brothers or family members. God's ways are not our ways!

God may assign you to care emotionally, spiritually, or physically for godly servants of God in their latter years. Look for opportunities to reach out to an elderly saint or parent who may now be the one who needs encouragement and love. God may want you to provide your home for them in their final years. Commit your heart to follow the Lord, and see how He blesses your life through others and, in turn, uses your life to bless those around you.

QUESTIONS FOR STUDY AND RESPONSE

1. God blessed Mary with several faithful women companions who helped her through the very difficult days after the loss of her Son. Has God placed some godly friends in your life who have helped you stay the course in your spiritual, emotional, and physical life?

2. It has always been God's plan to provide for the widows and the elderly. Do you have people in your life to whom God wants you to minister? Have you had the opportunity to honor your parents in this way?

3. Mary trusted the Lord in her times of tragedy and continued steadfastly in obedience. Instead of isolating herself, she sought the company of women who knew and loved her—or loved her Son. How do you respond when the difficult times come? Do you turn to the body of believers that He has provided for times like these, or do you seek isolation? Do you allow God to help you by using other Christian believers around you? Often God uses others in our lives to demonstrate His love for us in the physical sense—like a hug or a shoulder to lean on. If you find yourself in need, look for the one whom God will provide.

4. Scripturally, Mary is always depicted as living a life of quiet obedience, keeping all that the Lord had revealed safely in her heart. Are there encounters with the Lord that you have kept in your heart to remind you of God's love and watch-care for you?

5. With all the questions, pain, and sorrow in Mary's life, there is no hint of complaint, anger, or bitterness. She endured the suffering and death of her Son. Her lack of resentment toward God is so clearly shown through her testimony and experience to the early Church, as she continued with them in prayer and fellowship. Have you suffered a loss that left you feeling empty? Have you been able to keep your heart pure, trusting God to walk with you through the dark valleys of your life? Has your love for God grown through the challenges that have come your way? If you have allowed bitterness, anger, or resentment to cloud your relationship with God, confess it to Him, and He will restore your heart and life.

CHAPTER 12

SEEING A LIFE FROM GOD'S PERSPECTIVE

He who has My commandments and keeps them, it is he who loves
Me. And he who loves Me will be loved by My Father, and I will
love him and manifest Myself to him.
—JOHN 14:21

THERE ARE NO "SUPERSTARS" in God's kingdom. God and His Son are the sole focus. Because of this truth, God may have deliberately left Mary in obscurity after Acts 1. But our lives can benefit greatly from Mary's amazing example of utter faithfulness—especially through her challenges and struggles during the thirty-three years of Jesus' life. As we have carefully examined her life, we have discovered many principles and truths. Her initial response to God's invitation was one of absolute faith, but what her commitment and dedication would face, she could not possibly have known. Mary was vigilant to keep God's revelation and truths in her heart, and God continued to build upon her unwavering belief and trust in Him. She lived out her faith in the midst of family and other believers, being an example to all those around her. She was openly interdependent, which brought great encouragement to other believers.

Any person who "finds favor with God" is, and will be, greatly blessed, as we see in Mary's life. Each of us should look for God's love being uniquely expressed to us and live our lives with Mary's kind of faith and obedience.

WHAT CAN WE LEARN FROM MARY'S TESTIMONY?

To read and study the Scriptures is to encounter God. We learn of His nature, His ways, and both His eternal and His present purposes. We have stood steadily before God in His Word as we have looked at the life of Mary. And as we studied the Scripture, He revealed to us Himself and His ways as He chose, called, and used Mary's life. She was to be the earthly mother of the Son of God while He fulfilled His purpose to redeem the world. This journey has been, for us, profound and yet simple. So we now ask, What have we learned from looking at God's activity in and through Mary's life?

THE NATURE OF GOD

God is *holy*. God never compromises His holiness, even when He chooses ordinary people through whom to work. He looks for those whose hearts are completely loyal to Him (2 Chron. 16:9). And with Mary, God found someone who had "found favor with God" (Luke 1:30). That is, one whose character was approved of God. Mary's character proved to be true, as she responded immediately and in faith to God's announcement for her life.

God is *all knowing*. Nothing about any situation is beyond His purview or understanding. This is seen clearly when Herod made plans in "secret" to find and kill this "King of the Jews" (Jesus). Nothing can be hidden from God. What we do in secret God not only sees but exposes publicly (Mark 4:22). No enemy of God or God's people can work secretly without God knowing and intervening.

God is *all wise*. No man could have devised such a plan for the birth of His Son as we see in the life of Mary. There is nothing out of place and nothing lacking. The timing was perfect, and every detail was taken care of. All was ready and in place when God acted according to His wise purposes through Mary.

God is *all loving*. This is especially clear in God's relationship with Mary. His choices are in perfect love; His timing is in love; His ways are in inexpressible love; His eternal purposes are in perfect love; every aspect of His relationship with Mary is in perfect love. This is God's very nature. He would have to cease to be God not to express Himself in perfect love. Mary seemed to know this, and her faith expressed this. Her life was a constant expression of her faith in God's love.

God is a *rewarder* of those who diligently seek Him (Heb. 11:6). This is certainly seen in Simeon and Anna and the wise men. They were all earnestly and faithfully seeking God over a long period of time. In God's own time, He rewarded each of them in a personal and special way. They were rewarded for seeking Him with all their hearts. God had promised this in Jeremiah 29:13–14: "You will seek Me and find Me, when you search for Me with all your heart. I will be found by you, says the LORD." God affirmed this truth about His nature in Mary and all those associated with her.

The LORD looks from heaven; He sees all the sons of men. From the place of His dwelling He looks on all the inhabitants of the earth; He fashions their hearts individually; He considers all their works. (Ps. 33:13–15)

THE WAYS OF GOD

God gives thorough and daily guidance to those He chooses for His purposes. During the early years of Mary as a mother, God gave her and

Joseph very specific guidance and instruction, including timely warnings of danger. God also told them when and where to return from Egypt.

God uses ordinary people through whom to do His will. Mary was so very ordinary—and young. God chose ordinary shepherds to first reveal the Messiah's arrival. And Simeon and Anna were very ordinary and simple believers. There are countless other examples throughout Scripture and in our day of ordinary people who believed the Lord and were used in a mighty way.

God uses simple and ordinary places to do His greatest work in our world. Nazareth and Bethlehem, and not Jerusalem, were the arena of His working. A manger with no one present but maybe a few animals was chosen for the birth of His Son. How incredibly ordinary in the eyes of men, and in the eyes of history! Not a palace or the majestic and magnificent temple—but a lowly manger, for the greatest moment on God's agenda, in all of history. God used ordinary means to accomplish eternal and divine purposes.

God will always fulfill His promises. Mary allowed her life to become the fulfillment of centuries of prophecies given by God through many people. What God says, He does—and in great detail.

God does, indeed, enable those He calls. The moment Mary said yes to God, the Holy Spirit did "come upon" her and "the power of the Highest" did overshadow her (Luke 1:35), just as God had promised through the angel Gabriel. Every assignment from God that is accepted is always accompanied by God's enabling presence and power!

THE PURPOSES OF GOD

Eternity is always in the heart of God and in all He does. From eternity and *to* eternity is always on the heart of God and in the activity and purposes of God. This puts the setting or context of God's choices of those He calls as extremely important and eternally significant. Eternity is always in the heart of God as He works with His people. In other words, His timeline is much bigger than ours! Instead of just thinking and planning through our lifetime as we often do, He thinks through eternity. This is another reason that we should not be impatient while we wait on God's timing for something. His plans are so much greater than we can comprehend, and we must trust His timing and not our own. This is certainly true of Mary's life as she waited to see God fulfill His promise of Jesus' life.

A Testimony to God's Faithfulness
by Bobbye Rankin

Our arrival as missionaries in Indonesia in 1971 was the culmination of a lifelong dream. We knew beyond a shadow of doubt that we were called by God. Confidence was ours that God would bless our family of four, keep us healthy, and prosper us. Indeed His blessings were bountiful, but not in the way we expected. We had much to learn as we began our walk of faith cross-culturally.

After a year of language study, we were ready to conquer the world. Our first assignment was in East Java, four hours away from any other missionaries. As we eagerly settled into our new work, we expected to see a great movement of God among the Javanese people in our province.

To the contrary, we experienced many setbacks and saw little fruit. A promising church leader who was being trained to pastor one of the churches was jailed and later died in prison. Not only did we encounter unanticipated trials in ministry, but we faced a variety of health issues as well. A staphylococcus infection, resulting in boils, invaded our bodies. One evening we noticed an all-too-familiar pimple with red streaks on our two-year-old son's slightly swollen forehead. Instantly aware of the danger, we loaded the family in our Jeep and drove four hours to our Baptist hospital. Our son's swollen eyes were almost closed by the time we arrived at the emergency room. After a few days of heavy antibiotics, the doctors told us it was indeed fortunate that we brought him immediately to the hospital or he might not have lived.

While waiting for his recovery, we all had physical examinations. To my surprise it was advised that I have immediate major surgery. After three weeks of recuperation, we returned home just in time to celebrate our first Christmas in East Java. On December 26 I awoke with a high fever. Jerry followed suit two days later. Aspirin did nothing to deter the fever. Through consultation with our doctor by phone, we learned that we had contracted dengue, an acute, tropical viral disease transmitted by mosquitoes. The prognosis was that the fever would last for ten days, accompanied by severe joint pains. While Jerry and I spent most of the Christmas holidays in bed, our young daughter and son were cared for by loyal Indonesian friends.

On December 29 we received word that someone was trying to reach us by telephone. Jerry managed to walk to a neighbor's home where a working telephone was available. Upon his return he gave me the incomprehensible news that my parents had been in an automobile accident in Mississippi. My father had been killed immediately, and my mother was in critical condition. At that moment, lacking the physical and emotional energy to comprehend the shocking news, I felt so alone, isolated from everyone, including the Lord.

In His precise timing, God supplied our needs. The next day, having driven a long distance, three colleagues arrived at our home. They packed our belongings and made travel plans to America for me and the children. Not knowing if my mother would live or die, I was confident that seeing her grandchildren after a long separation would be a blessing and might even speed her recovery.

Upon arrival in America, I immediately went to my mother's

hospital room. That first evening after she went to sleep, I knelt by her hospital bed. Fully intending to ask the Lord to heal and extend her life, it seemed unnecessary to ask Him for anything. For the first time in a long, silent season, I was made aware that His presence was powerfully with me. His love and peace seemed to enfold and fill me with an inexplicable joy. Worship was my only response. That "dark night of my soul" was being transformed into a deeper intimacy with Him. Confirmation came that I was in His will and that He had a divine purpose in everything He had allowed in our lives.

The words of Isaiah 41:9–10 convey what the Lord said to me during that loving encounter with Him: "You whom I have taken from the ends of the earth, and called from its farthest regions, and said to you, 'You are My servant, I have chosen you and have not cast you away: Fear not, for I am with you; be not dismayed, for I am your God. I will strengthen you, yes, I will help you, I will uphold you with My righteous right hand.'" Faithful is He in all His ways! My mother lived an additional twenty-eight years in good health.

As I reflect on those early years on the mission field, I clearly see that God was preparing my heart and life for future service. I had so much to learn! Growth was essential in order to be an obedient, usable vessel whatever the season. I was reminded of Mrs. Baker James Cauthen's comments at our appointment service. She looked us in the eye and said, "You have lived a charmed life." Later I came to understand that she was referring to our life histories, which indicated few major struggles. It was as if she were saying, "Be ready, insurmountable challenges will come, which can only be met in and through the power of God." And come they did!

During that first term I came to truly understand, through firsthand experience, that God was faithful in all His ways and that nothing would touch me or my family that was not permitted or preordained by Him. That realization has been a strong anchor in my life. He placed within my heart a longing to know Him intimately and to spend early morning hours in His Word, listening to His voice. God was preparing me for greater challenges to come. I would never have dreamed that my husband would be placed by God in a place of leadership that would take us away from the field.

I have found myself thanking Him in the past few years for every trial that He led us through. In each seemingly hopeless situation, His presence and His Word have brought clarity and joy in the midst of difficulties. I have found that the furnace of adversity and the fountain of joy are inexplicably one.

It has been a joy for Marilynn and me (Henry) to have had the opportunity to travel and lead many conferences all over the world with the Rankins. Bobbye's deep love for God's Word and her commitment to the Lord is always in evidence. When we were thinking of those God placed around our lives who always strove to be obedient, we thought of her example to us and to the many missionaries she has encouraged all over the world—including Carrie.

God eternally loves as He encounters those whom He chooses and those who wholly obey Him. Jesus indicated this clearly when He said, "He who has My commandments and keeps them, it is he who loves Me. And he who loves Me will be loved by My Father, and I will love him and manifest Myself to him" (John 14:21). God cannot act contrary to His very nature. So Mary, throughout her life, experienced the perfect and complete love of God. Everything in Mary's life can (and should) be seen in terms of God's love—including the Cross.

Faith is clearly evident in the purposes of God. This was true not only in Mary's life and in Joseph's life, but also in Zacharias's and Elizabeth's lives, in Simeon and Anna, and even in the shepherds and the wise men who searched as God was indicating. Each of these walked by faith, believing the promises of God, and experienced God working fully through their lives. Throughout Scripture God indicates over and over again that without faith, it is impossible to please God (Heb. 11:6).

Also, Jesus said clearly, "If you have faith . . . nothing will be impossible for you" (Matt. 17:20). And further, "Have faith in God . . . whatever things you ask when you pray, believe that you receive them, and you will have them" (Mark 11:22–24).

It is in the eternal purposes of God that all should relate to Him in faith.

WHAT WE CAN LEARN FROM MARY

There are many truths that we can learn from Mary's life, especially in her responses to God. We need to apply these to our lives today.

Obedience is crucial, opening our lives to the amazing workings of God. No matter how dramatic the encounter is with God, if it is not followed by immediate and thorough obedience, nothing will change or happen in our lives with God. But immediate and simple obedience in ordinary people brings the full presence and activity of God. And God's activity will bless others' lives immeasurably in the process.

Mary's expression of faith is one of the greatest responses to God in the entire Bible. "Behold the maidservant of the Lord! Let it be to me according to your word" (Luke 1:38).

Everything that God did in Mary's life proceeded from her absolute faith in God. We see that there are no arguments from Mary, no delays, and no complaints. Though she often "kept all these things and pondered them in her heart" (Luke 2:19), there is never even a hint of doubt! Her relationship to God and His will was settled. Mary possessed complete trust in the Lord and proceeded to experience God unfolding His eternal purposes in and through her life.

Mary's faith was expressed by what Eugene Peterson calls "the long obedience in the same direction." No evidence of hesitation, just obedience. Immediate obedience in faith has always been the key to anyone and everyone experiencing God. To know what God is wanting for you and to choose not to obey is sin (James 4:17). When there is sin in our lives, everything that God is doing in our lives will cease (Ps. 66:18; Isa. 59:1–2).

Mary and Joseph constantly obeyed the laws, statutes, and judgments of God. Every year at the commanded times, Mary and Joseph fulfilled the Word of God faithfully. From the earliest days in Jesus' life, Mary and Joseph obeyed the Laws and commands of God (Luke 2:21–24). Their obedience was lived out daily before Jesus, throughout His life (Luke 2:41). Jesus knew and watched their obedience, allowing it to affect His obedience as well.

It seems also that Mary never lost the wonder of all that God was doing in her life. Each step of her spiritual pilgrimage she walked in "wonder." We have mentioned several times that "His mother kept all these things in her heart" (Luke 2:51). Those whom God chooses and calls, who respond in obedience, never seem to lose the wonder of this special relationship with God. The apostle Paul never lost this sense of wonder as he walked faithfully before the Lord (1 Tim. 1:15–17), and we as God's people should not lose this either. It is an amazing thing to be chosen by God for His special purposes, and we should never forget the wonder of the opportunity to be blessed by Him.

Mary had good and helpful companions to lean on, especially after the death of her husband, Joseph. Women became her trusted companions, walking with her through her most troubling times. And at Jesus' word from the cross, she let the apostle John look after her in all her needs to the end of her life (John 19:27). Mary was not a "loner," even though she was special to God. She wisely walked with fellow believers who watched over her and encouraged her to live out her life of faith.

In Mary there is no evidence of complaining or doubting. Her life was both ordinary and unique. She had bewildering moments (Luke 2:50) and incredibly painful moments—but there is no mention of her complaining. Faith does not complain, but trusts!

In the background of Mary's life is a marriage of unity. Mary and Joseph walked with one heart and one mind as they did the will of God—and as God worked His purposes through them. One must linger at each moment where it is recorded that they did or experienced something *together*. God works in the hearts of all who are vitally related to the ones He chooses and calls, working in and through them both. Harmony in marriage is essential for God to work and be honored in any individual's life and work. This was true with Mary and Joseph, and this is true for us today.

A UNIFIED CALLING

There is no way that I (Carrie) could be following God's plan for my life if God had not also called my husband to the same task. If our hearts were not completely united in our ministry, there would be no possibility for God to complete His purposes through our lives. Can you imagine what it would be like on the mission field if only one was committed to the call? Eventually, the one without the calling could not take the pressures of living in another culture and would become resentful of giving up family, position, wealth, and the chance to live in a comfortable and familiar environment. Problems with children could be blamed on the other for bringing them to another culture. The problems would be endless, the ministry would be stilted, and the marriage could shatter.

God's choice of Mary included His choice of Joseph. They needed each other to complete God's task for them as they followed God's direction for their lives.

Tragedies and sorrows did not turn Mary aside from God's will and purposes in her life. She lost her husband, possibly while Jesus was a teenager. Then she lost her eldest son, her firstborn, in a most unfair and cruel death on a cross while many mocked Him. She could have turned away from God and His will for her, as many seem to do when tragedy strikes. Too often, if a couple loses a child, their marriage ends in divorce, and one or both may turn away from God in anger or bitterness. Not so with Mary. She continued in the midst of God's people and was with them when they were all "filled with the Holy Spirit" (Acts 2:1–4). There is no hint of bitterness or anger in Mary—only confident faith.

WHAT ELSE CAN WE LEARN FROM SCRIPTURE?

THERE IS UNITY IN THE SCRIPTURES

From Genesis 3:15, when God spoke about His ultimate victory over Satan and sin, throughout the rest of the Old Testament, to the vital quotes in the Gospels connecting the events in Mary's life and Jesus' life, Scripture has one message: God loved the world and gave His Son for the world to bring all people back to Himself after they fall into sin. Scripture is prominent throughout Mary and Jesus' lives.

SCRIPTURE IS GOD'S MEANS TO KEEP HIS PEOPLE INFORMED OF HIS WAYS AND PURPOSES

Every child of God can walk in assurance and peace and harmony with God, as Mary and Jesus did from the Scripture. Everything we need to help us find and experience Him is provided in the Scripture!

THE HARMONY FOUND IN SCRIPTURE AND REVEALED IN GOD'S RELATIONSHIP WITH MARY IS ENCOURAGING AND SUBSTANTIAL

God was exactly the same with Mary as He had been from the beginning of time and throughout the centuries. His dealing with others as He chose them, loved them, and accomplished His eternal purposes through them was the same with Mary—and works the same in those He chooses and loves in our day also.

GOD'S REQUIREMENTS OF FAITH IN HISTORY AND IN MARY'S LIFE ARE THE SAME TODAY

There is unity and harmony in the Scriptures that reveal God and how He works with those He chooses, like Mary. The Scriptures also reveal the presence and work of the Holy Spirit in Mary and in Jesus, and in us also.

THE SCRIPTURES REVEAL THE CRUCIAL PLACE OF OBEDIENCE AS AN EXPRESSION OF FAITH

In each one, and especially in Mary, obedience unlocks the powerful activity of God in every life. This is a clear and simple truth that a child can understand: The one who obeys is the one God will use. These Scriptures bring this out simply and clearly.

LASTLY, THE SCRIPTURES ALSO TEACH US THE ESSENTIAL ROLE OF THE HUSBAND IN EVERY MARRIAGE

The prophet Malachi prophesied, "Before the coming of the great and dreadful day of the LORD [the coming of the Messiah] . . . he [John the Baptist] will turn the hearts of the fathers to the children, and the hearts of the children to their fathers" (Mal. 4:5–6).

Joseph was an extremely faithful husband to Mary and father to Jesus. He walked faithfully with God, both hearing and obeying every word from God. God chose to speak to Joseph several times to bring safety to

Mary and Jesus, and his walk with God was crucial, and even life-saving for Jesus—such as when the angel warned him to take Mary and Jesus into Egypt to escape the wrath and terror and death spread on multitudes of helpless babies and young children. Joseph again heard from God as God led him to know when and where they were to return from Egypt (Matt. 2:19–23).

THE CONSEQUENCES FOR NOT RESPONDING TO GOD IN IMMEDIATE OBEDIENCE

When God encounters His children and gives a clear command or directive, this is life's most significant moment. To say no to God or to fail to obey Him is most serious to God. The cost or consequences from such actions are measureless, for they affect eternity! Would you dare refuse to respond to a serious word from a king or queen, or the president of the United States? No. That would be an affront to the nation they represent. How much greater is the offense of saying no to God. God is God and not man! To say no is an offense against all of heaven. Saying no to God is sin!

> **Would you dare refuse to respond to a serious word from a king or queen, or the president of the United States? . . . How much greater is the offense of saying no to God. God is God and not man! To say no is an offense against all of heaven. Saying no to God is sin!**

A picture of the serious consequences from God can be seen throughout the Scripture. Deuteronomy 30:11–20 tells us that to fail to "hear" and obey God's voice and return to worship only Him will result in death. God gave His people a choice of life or death (Deut. 30:15), of living a life of blessing or cursing. In many ways this is true in our day. God gives us opportunities for living a life of obedience and experiencing the wonder of His wisdom and power, or living a life without knowing the God we proclaim to serve. For God was talking to His own people in this passage. He leaves the choice of our involvement up to us.

Jesus also said to those of His people who were rebelling against God, "I tell you . . . unless you repent you will all likewise perish" (Luke 13:5). Jesus knew how serious it was for God's people not to obey Him.

In Matthew 13 Jesus illustrated that how we receive a word from God will determine if we will "bear fruit." Jesus also said that it was "by this My Father is glorified, that you bear much fruit; so you will be My disciples" (John 15:8). A hard heart, a shallow heart, or a totally distracted heart is like soil receiving seed but not bearing fruit. However, immediate obedience, like Mary's, would bear fruit and be pleasing to God.

A further consequence to not obeying God is given in the parable of the Vine and the branch in John 15. "Every branch in Me that does not bear fruit He takes away . . . and they gather them and throw them into the fire, and they are burned" (vv. 2, 6).

There are several instances in which the Scripture mentions a hardening of hearts. When Pharaoh would not heed God's Word to Him, his heart was hardened (Exo. 8:15). The writer of Hebrews warned God's people, "Today, if you will hear His voice, do not harden your hearts" (Heb. 3:15). This warning is thorough and with real consequences. A hardened heart never receives God's promises!

The most comprehensive statement of cost and consequences for disobedience by God's people is stated by God in His covenant promise to His people in Deuteronomy 28. For fourteen verses God promises great blessings on those who obey Him. Then throughout the next forty-one verses, He states in detail how God would deal with disobedience when He gave commands.

When God called men to be prophets to His people, He gave them an urgent message. "You, My people, must repent of your sins. You are now at a crisis—you can have revival by returning to Me; or you will perish!" The heart of God was always very tender toward His covenant people. Through His servant Ezekiel, a watchman on the walls for His people (see Ezek. 33:7), God announced His heart:

> "But when a righteous man turns away from his righteousness and commits iniquity, and does according to all the abominations that the wicked man does, shall he live? All the righteousness which he has done shall not be remembered; because of the unfaithfulness of which he is guilty and the sin which he has committed, because of them he shall die . . . Therefore I will judge you, O house of Israel, every one according to his ways," says the Lord GOD. "Repent, and turn from all your transgressions, so that iniquity will not be your ruin. Cast away from you all the transgressions which you have committed, and get yourselves a new heart and a new spirit. For why should you die, O house of Israel? For I have no pleasure in the death of one who dies," says the Lord GOD. "Therefore turn and live!" (Ezek. 18:24, 30–32)

God always desired fullness of life for His people. But their refusal to obey Him and their turning to idols and other abominations brought them to destruction. Israel refused the prophets, and God destroyed them in 722 B.C. Judah refused to obey God's Word to them through the prophets, and they were destroyed in 586 B.C. and taken into captivity in Babylon for seventy years. In Jesus' day He had to pronounce destruction on that favored city of God by the Romans in 72 A.D.

When the people of God individually or corporately refuse to obey God, the consequences are clear and devastating. God sanctifies His name (Ezek. 36:23) before a watching world when God's people profane His name before the nations. God has clearly revealed His ways for His people. We are without excuse, if we know His will and refuse to do it!

We have clearly stated the blessings that came upon Mary as she obeyed over her lifetime, once she knew God's will for her. We felt it was necessary to also give what God said He would do if His people knew His voice and His will and failed to obey Him.

It is important to encounter God in His Word, especially as He works in individuals like Mary. When you encounter God through the Word, God will open your understanding and passages will become clear. Words that you've read in the Bible many times now show you a deeper meaning. Your heart may quicken with excitement, or you may have a deep burden because of sin in your life. This is God revealing Himself and His ways.

The purpose of Scripture is not merely for information about God and the people through whom He has worked, but to lead us to experience God in our own lives. To know and experience God is life's greatest blessing. To then respond in faith and obedience opens our lives to God's activity. And all this gives our lives an eternal significance, bringing a deep, real motivation to live our lives intentionally and with hope.

In all our awareness of Mary's responses to God, through very difficult and challenging circumstance, we know of no doubts or complaining throughout her walk with the Lord. She chose to trust God and not to question God in doubt. Faith is the basis for a confident walk with God. Mary has helped us first to examine our faith in God and then to weigh our walk with God. It is our responsibility to know if our hearts are right before the Lord. When we seek to stand blameless before the Lord, He will show us the way to cleanse our life through Christ.

Although the Scriptures give us limited knowledge of Mary's life, we do see her life in the larger context of God's eternal purposes. It is not always the extensiveness of God's activity in us but the eternal context of His activity that gives significance for our lives. We could be a part of something the Lord wants to do to bring His purposes to completion in our country and throughout the world. If we choose, this truth alone can give us a real sense of purpose for living out our lives. May God grant us such awareness. Once God chooses to show His favor and allow us to experience Him, no external circumstance can prevent Him from completing His work through us.

Several times throughout this book, we have made reference to Mary's pure heart. The Bible often mentions that God is looking for a person with a pure heart. But what does this mean for us today?

A *pure heart* is one that is cleansed by "the washing of water by the word" (Eph. 5:26). When we spend time thoroughly immersed in God's Word and we repent, we are cleansed by God. God uses His Word to reveal Himself and His ways. He then draws us to Himself, and we are transformed into His likeness in this process (2 Cor. 3:18). We then must live out our daily life, being constantly conformed to the image of Christ (Rom. 8:28–30). In the simplest terms, seek to apply all that God teaches you. When you fail or when the Scripture reveals that you have not obeyed, immediately ask for forgiveness and repent. Don't wait! Commit your ways and your heart to Him, and your life will look more like Christ every day. This is what being a Christian is all about. This is the example that God gave to us in the form of Mary. God took an ordinary life that was yielded to Him and used her to make an extraordinary impact on history.

God is still working today, looking for the life that He can trust with His work. We have shown several examples of ordinary women who have yielded their lives in commitment to the Lord. He, in turn, has used each individually where He's placed them, and their lives have never been the same. When we approached each person about including a testimony of an encounter with the Lord, they all had several that they could have written, but they chose the one they felt God wanted them to include.

Many did not have a complete vision of what God wanted to accomplish when He encountered them, but it took years to see the full purpose of their obedience and what God wanted to achieve. Some had to trust the Lord through some very dark and difficult times. Others had to trust that God was sovereign and that His will for their lives is perfect. They each discovered that it is the daily walk with the Lord, both the small and large steps, that brought them closer to God and created the opportunity to be of use in His kingdom purposes.

Please evaluate your life and take an honest look at your heart before the Lord. Are you willing to commit your ways to the Lord? Are you willing to trust in His wisdom for you and your family? Do you want to see God work personally in your life? If you answered yes, then you are well on your way to seeing the Lord work through you! God wants to use your life, just like He used Mary's, to bless others around you. Your life, like Mary's, can be a blessing if you choose to obey.

QUESTIONS FOR STUDY AND RESPONSE

1. Mary's faith in God began early in her life and continued through-out her days. She pondered the things God taught her and always held them close to her heart. Learning from her example, have you carefully kept track of your encounters with the Lord? Have you written a thorough record of when your faith first began? Have you grown in your faith since then?

2. God chose to reveal Himself, His ways, and His purposes to Mary once she was chosen and called. He even gave her (and Joseph) step-by-step guidance. What specifically has God revealed to you about His nature, His ways, His purposes, and how He wants to use your life?

3. Mary clearly responded to all of God's activity in and around her life by obediently following all of His commands. How have you responded to God? Can you always be found with an obedient heart?

4. When we choose to be disobedient to what God has revealed to us, there are consequences that can be far-reaching. For Mary, she could have missed the complete revelation of the Holy Spirit if she had allowed her life to fall into bitterness after Jesus' death. This would have brought far-reaching consequences to her family, who later all came to know Jesus as Lord and not just as a brother. Have you seen the effects of your obedience on your family? Have you

seen any consequences in your family to disobedience in your own walk with God? If so, ask God's forgiveness and repent. He will restore your relationship to Him and use your life for His purposes.

5. The Scriptures never record Mary expressing her doubt or disbelief in God. We do not take that to mean that she was sinless, yet she is left to us as an example of one who was completely obedient in the midst of all of her life's circumstances. As you examine your own heart, have you ever expressed doubt about what God has revealed in your life? Have you ever felt abandoned in the midst of a difficult circumstance? Take heart from understanding how thoroughly God took care of Mary, and know that His love for you is the same! Ask Him to forgive your doubt, and you will again be able to deeply experience His presence.

6. If God comes to your life today, are you prepared to respond to Him with a pure heart, immediately seeking to be obedient to all He has commanded? Are you willing to allow God to change your life and the life of your family so that you can be a part of God's eternal purposes? He will use your life and your obedience to be the vessel of blessing to accomplish His purposes in our day.

7. We have included many testimonies to God's faithfulness in our lives and in the lives of those who have traveled this journey beside us—faithful companions and friends to whom God has joined our lives. Have any of the stories struck a chord in your own life? Can you identify with their encounter with the Lord? God intended for us to learn from others so that we can grow deeper in our walk with the Lord together. As these women included in the book have

faithfully shared God's work in their lives, we have the same obligation and commitment. When you meet together for fellowship or study, commit to sharing God's faithfulness with one another. God will unite our hearts as we focus on Him and what He's doing in and through our lives.

NOTES

Chapter 1

1. G. Campbell Morgan, *The Gospel According to Luke* (NY: Revell, 1931), 20.

2. Ibid., 19.

3. Howard F. Vos, *Nelson's New Illustrated Bible Manners & Customs: How People of the Bible Really Lived* (Nashville, TN: Thomas Nelson, 1999), 449.

4. There are many interesting books and biographies on both contemporary and historical women. *All the Women of the Bible*, by Herbert Lockyer, would be helpful as well as books on Condoleezza Rice, Beth Moore, Anne Graham Lotz, Bertha Smith, Elizabeth Elliot, and others that give a testimony to their walk with the Lord.

Chapter 2

1. Doug Greenwold, *Zechariah & Elizabeth: Persistent Faith in a Faithful God* (Rockville, MD: Bible in Context Ministries, 2004), 13.

2. Ibid., 10.

3. Leon Morris, *Tyndale New Testament Commentaries: Luke* (Leicester, England: Intervarsity Press, 1999), 75.

4. Howard F. Vos, *Nelson's New Illustrated Bible Manners & Customs: How People of the Bible Really Lived* (Nashville, TN: Thomas Nelson, 1999), 450.

5. Morris, *Tyndale New Testament Commentaries: Luke*, 75.

6. Greenwold, *Zechariah & Elizabeth*, 21.

7. Read Luke 1:67–79 to have a clear picture of Zacharias's heart as he is overwhelmed at all God is doing.

Chapter 3

1. Howard F. Vos, *Nelson's New Illustrated Bible Manners & Customs: How People of the Bible Really Lived* (Nashville, TN: Thomas Nelson, 1999), 450.

2. Alfred Edersheim, *Sketches of Jewish Social Life in the Days of Christ* (Grand Rapids, MI: Eerdmans, 1957), 105.

3. Ibid., 106.

4. Vos, *Nelson's New Illustrated Bible Manners & Customs*, 450.

Chapter 4

1. Howard F. Vos, *Nelson's New Illustrated Bible Manners & Customs: How People of the Bible Really Lived* (Nashville, TN: Thomas Nelson, 1999), 383.

2. Vos, *Nelson's New Illustrated Bible Manners & Customs*, 345.

3. Henry Halley, *Halley's Bible Handbook* (Grand Rapids, MI: Zondervan, 2000), 649.

Chapter 5

1. For more on this topic, see the Biblical Legacy series book on Samuel called *Chosen to Be God's Prophet: Lessons from the Life of Samuel—How God Works in and Through Those He Chooses* by Henry Blackaby (Nashville, TN: Thomas Nelson, 2003).

Chapter 7

1. Later, God would use this song against the children of Israel in judgment. Although they knew of the mighty works of God on their behalf through the singing of this song, they turned to evil and all that was corrupt before their Lord. See Deut. 31ff.

2. Leon Morris, *Tyndale New Testament Commentaries: Luke* (Leicester, England: Intervarsity Press, 1999), 84.

3. Ibid.

4. We have included their music book *Return to Me: A Fresh Encounter with God Through Song* in the Bibliography of this book.

5. Robert J. Morgan, *Then Sings My Soul: 150 of the World's Greatest Hymn Stories* (Nashville, TN: Nelson Bible & Reference, 2003), 184.

6. Ibid., 183.

7. Ibid., 175.

8. Ibid., 195.

Chapter 8

1. Leon Morris, *Tyndale New Testament Commentaries: Luke* (Leicester, England: Intervarsity Press, 1999), 94.

2. Ibid., 93.

3. David Brown, *A Commentary: Critical, Experimental and Practical on the Old and New Testaments: Vol. V* (Grand Rapids, MI: Eerdmans, 1948), 4.

4. Charles Erdman, *The Gospel of Matthew* (Philadelphia, PN: The Westminster Press, 1977), 33.

5. Ibid., 34.

6. Howard F. Vos, *Nelson's New Illustrated Bible Manners & Customs: How People of the Bible Really Lived* (Nashville, TN: Thomas Nelson, 1999), 396.

7. Ibid., 401.

8. Ibid., 392.

9. Ibid., 401.

10. G. Campbell Morgan, *The Gospel According to Luke* (New York, NY: Revell, 1931), 42.

11. Ibid., 97.

12. Morris, *Tyndale New Testament Commentaries: Luke*, 99.

Chapter 9

1. G. Campbell Morgan, *The Gospel According to Luke* (New York, NY: Revell, 1931), 36.

2. Ibid., 43.

3. Howard F. Vos, *Nelson's New Illustrated Bible Manners & Customs: How People of the Bible Really Lived* (Nashville, TN: Thomas Nelson, 1999), 451.

4. Ibid., 452.

5. Ibid., 451.

6. It is a common belief that the wise men came after this time, which did give Mary and Joseph enough wealth to escape and flee into Egypt (Morgan, *The Gospel According to Luke*, 42).

7. Vos, *Nelson's New Illustrated Bible Manners & Customs*, 451.

8. Morgan, *The Gospel According to Luke*, 44.

9. Morris, *Tyndale New Testament Commentaries: Luke*, 100.

10. Ibid., 100.

11. Morgan, *The Gospel According to Luke*, 43.

Chapter 10

1. Leon Morris, *Tyndale New Testament Commentaries: Luke* (Leicester, England: Intervarsity Press, 1999), 111.

2. Ibid.

3. Howard F. Vos, *Nelson's New Illustrated Bible Manners & Customs: How People of the Bible Really Lived* (Nashville, TN: Thomas Nelson, 1999), 464.

4. Leon Morris, *Reflections on the Gospel of John* (Peabody, MA: Hendrickson, 2000), 71.

5. Ibid., 70.

6. Ibid., 72.

BIBLIOGRAPHY

Brown, David, Robert Jamieson, and A. R. Fausset. *A Commentary: Critical, Experimental and Practical on the Old and New Testaments: Vol. V.* Grand Rapids, MI: Eerdmans, 1948.

Edersheim, Alfred. *Sketches of Jewish Social Life in the Days of Christ.* Grand Rapids, MI: Eerdmans, 1957.

Erdman, Charles. *The Gospel of Matthew.* Philadelphia, PA: Westminster Press, 1977.

France, R. T., *Tyndale New Testament Commentaries: Matthew.* Leicester, England: Intervarsity Press, 1999.

Greenwold, Doug. *Zechariah & Elizabeth: Persistent Faith in a Faithful God.* Rockville, MD: Bible in Context Ministries, 2004.

Halley, Henry. *Halley's Bible Handbook.* Grand Rapids, MI: Zondervan, 2000.

Lockyer, Herbert. *All the Women of the Bible.* Grand Rapids, MI: Zondervan, 1967.

Morgan, G. Campbell. *The Gospel According to Luke.* New York, NY: Revell, 1931.

Morgan, Robert J. *Then Sings My Soul: 150 of the World's Greatest Hymn Stories.* Nashville, TN: Thomas Nelson, 2003.

Morris, Leon. *Reflections on the Gospel of John.* Peabody, MA: Hendrickson, 2000.

———. *Tyndale New Testament Commentaries: Luke.* Leicester, England: Intervarsity Press, 1999.

The Nelson Study Bible. Nashville, TN: Thomas Nelson, 1997.

Owens, Ron and Patricia. *Return to Me: A Fresh Encounter with God Through Song.* Nashville, TN: Lifeway, 1993.

Vos, Howard F. *Nelson's New Illustrated Bible Manners & Customs.* Nashville, TN: Thomas Nelson, 1999.

ABOUT THE AUTHORS

Henry Blackaby is the author of more than a dozen books, including the best-selling *Experiencing God* Bible studies. Dr. Blackaby is a graduate of the University of British Columbia, Vancouver, Canada. He has completed his Th.M. degree from Golden Gate Baptist Theological Seminary. He has also received four honorary doctorate degrees and is now serving as the president of Henry Blackaby Ministries. Dr. Blackaby and his wife, Marilynn, have five married children, all serving in Christian ministry. They are also blessed with fourteen grandchildren.

Carrie Blackaby Webb is the youngest child of Henry and Marilynn Blackaby. Carrie has worked on staff in several different churches in the areas of music and worship, children's ministry, and youth work. She and her husband, Wendell, are currently serving as career missionaries in Germany as team leaders and strategy coordinators for the Hochsauerland region. They have two children, Elizabeth and Joshua.

ACKNOWLEDGMENTS

WE WOULD BOTH LIKE to express our deepest appreciation to Jan Robertson for all her time and input on editing this project. Also, our heartfelt dedication goes to all the women who granted us a look into their hearts, allowing us to see how God has encountered and changed their lives. Your obedience is an inspiration: Minette Drumwright Pratt, Patricia Owens, Jan Johnsonius, Marilynn Blackaby, Gina Blackaby, Linda Hokit, Pam Kirkland, Jan Carter, Julie Cook, Jan Robertson, Bobbye Rankin, Karen O'Dell Bullock, and Anne Graham Lotz.